Qualifications and Credit Framework (QCF)
LEVEL 3 DIPLOMA IN ACCOUNTING

TEXT

Indirect Tax

FA 2009

2010 Edition

First edition July 2010

Printed text ISBN 9780 7517 8562 3

British Library Cataloguing-in-Publication Data
A catalogue record for this book is available from the British
Library

Published by

BPP Learning Media Ltd
BPP House
Aldine Place
London
W12 8AA

www.bpp.com/learningmedia

Printed in the United Kingdom

CONTENTS

A NOTE ABOUT COPYRIGHT

Dear Customer

What does the little © mean and why does it matter?

Your market-leading BPP books, course materials and e-learning materials do not write and update themselves. People write them: on their own behalf or as employees of an organisation that invests in this activity. Copyright law protects their livelihoods. It does so by creating rights over the use of the content.

Breach of copyright is a form of theft – as well as being a criminal offence in some jurisdictions, it is potentially a serious breach of professional ethics.

With current technology, things might seem a bit hazy but, basically, without the express permission of BPP Learning Media:

- Photocopying our materials is a breach of copyright

- Scanning, ripcasting or conversion of our digital materials into different file formats, uploading them to facebook or emailing them to your friends is a breach of copyright

You can, of course, sell your books, in the form in which you have bought them – once you have finished with them. (Is this fair to your fellow students? We update for a reason.)

And what about outside the UK? BPP Learning Media strives to make our materials available at prices students can afford by local printing arrangements, pricing policies and partnerships which are clearly listed on our website. A tiny minority ignore this and indulge in criminal activity by illegally photocopying our material or supporting organisations that do. If they act illegally and unethically in one area, can you really trust them?

INTRODUCTION

This is a time of great change for the AAT. From 1 July 2010 the AAT's assessments will fall within the **Qualifications and Credit Framework** and most papers will be assessed by way of an on demand **computer based assessment**. BPP Learning Media has reacted to this change by investing heavily to produce new ground breaking market leading resources. In particular, our **new suite of online resources** ensures that you are prepared for online testing by means of an online environment where tasks mimic the style of the AAT's assessment tasks.

The BPP range of resources comprises:

- **Texts**, covering all the knowledge and understanding needed by you, with numerous illustrations of 'how it works', practical examples and tasks for you to use to consolidate your learning. The majority of tasks within the texts have been written in an interactive style that reflects the style of the online tasks the AAT will set. Texts are available in our traditional paper format and, in addition, as E books which can be downloaded to your PC or laptop.

- **Question Banks**, including additional learning questions plus the AAT's practice assessment and a number of other full practice assessments. Full answers to all questions and assessments, prepared by BPP Learning Media Ltd, are included. For the first time our question banks are available in an online environment which mimics the AAT's testing environment. This enables you to familiarise yourself with the environment in which you will be tested

- **Passcards,** which are handy pocket sized revision tools designed to fit in a handbag or briefcase to enable students to revise anywhere at anytime. All major points are covered in the passcards which have been designed to assist you in consolidating knowledge

- **Workbooks,** which have been designed to cover the units that are assessed by way of project/case study. The workbooks contain many practical tasks to assist in the learning process and also a sample assessment or project to work through.

- **Lecturers' resources**, providing a further bank of tasks, answers and full practice assessments for classroom use, available separately only to lecturers whose colleges adopt BPP Learning Media material. The lecturers resources are available in both paper format and online in E format.

This Text for Indirect Tax has been written specifically to ensure comprehensive yet concise coverage of the AAT's new learning outcomes and assessment criteria. It is fully up to date as at June 2010 and reflects both the AAT's unit guide and the practice assessment provided by the AAT.

Each chapter contains:

- clear, step by step explanation of the topic

- logical progression and linking from one chapter to the next

- numerous illustrations of 'how it works'

- interactive tasks within the text of the chapter itself, with answers at the back of the book. In general, these tasks have been written in the interactive form that students will see in their real assessments

- test your learning questions of varying complexity, again with answers supplied at the back of the book. In general these test questions have been written in the interactive form that students will see in their real assessments

The emphasis in all tasks and test questions is on the practical application of the skills acquired.

If you have any comments about this book, please e-mail suedexter@bpp.com or write to Sue Dexter, Publishing Director, BPP Learning Media Ltd, BPP House, Aldine Place, London W12 8AA.

A NOTE ABOUT VAT

There was a change in the standard rate of VAT from 15% to 17.5% on 1 January 2010. However, in accordance with the guidance issued by AAT, when calculating VAT you should always use a standard rate of 17.5% regardless of the date of the transaction.

ASSESSMENT STRATEGY

Indirect Tax (ITX) is the only tax assessment at level 3.

ITX is a 90 minute assessment. The assessment material will normally be provided by the AAT, delivered online and assessed locally. If additional reference material is required, details will be provided in advance of the assessment.

The ITX assessment consists of six tasks, five in Section 1 and one in Section 2.

Section 1 will comprise five short-answer tasks assessing the learner's knowledge of the principles of VAT and their ability to understand and interpret VAT guidance given to them. Some simple calculations will be required. A number of the tasks will be multiple-choice or true/false statements.

Section 2 will comprise one task. This will require the completion of a VAT return from information extracted from the accounting system, followed by a short piece of communication to an internal or external person.

Competency

Learners will be required to demonstrate competence in both sections of the assessment. For the purpose of assessment the competency level for AAT assessment is set at 70 per cent. The level descriptor in the table below describes the ability and skills students at this level must successfully demonstrate to achieve competence.

QCF Level descriptor	Summary
	Achievement at level 3 reflects the ability to identify and use relevant understanding, methods and skills to complete tasks and address problems that, while well defined, have a measure of complexity. It includes taking responsibility for initiating and completing tasks and procedures as well as exercising autonomy and judgement within limited parameters. It also reflects awareness of different perspectives or approaches within an area of study or work.

Knowledge and understanding

- Use factual, procedural and theoretical understanding to complete tasks and address problems that, while well defined, may be complex and non-routine

- Interpret and evaluate relevant information and ideas

- Be aware of the nature of the area of study or work

- Have awareness of different perspectives or approaches within the area of study or work

Application and action

- Address problems that, while well defined, may be complex and non routine

- Identify, select and use appropriate skills, methods and procedures

- Use appropriate investigation to inform actions

- Review how effective methods and actions have been

Autonomy and accountability

- Take responsibility for initiating and completing tasks and procedures, including, where relevant, responsibility for supervising or guiding others

- Exercise autonomy and judgement within limited parameters

AAT UNIT GUIDE

Indirect Tax

Introduction

Please read this document in conjunction with the standards for the unit.

Successful completion of this AAT learning and assessment area will result in the award of two QCF units:

- Preparing and completing VAT returns (skills)
- Principles of VAT (knowledge)

The purpose of the unit

The unit is designed to ensure that learners can understand basic VAT regulations, accurately complete VAT returns, and communicate VAT information to relevant people. As VAT is subject to specific and detailed regulations, the learner should be able to seek guidance from relevant sources, process what is found and communicate this to others.

Learning objectives

After successful completion of this unit, the learner will be able to deal with the most commonly occurring VAT issues in a business. Although some basic knowledge will be expected, the emphasis is not so much on recall as on awareness and understanding. The learner will be aware that regulations exist and know how to find the information to ensure that the business complies with the regulations and avoids surcharges and penalties. The learner will be able to extract information from the relevant source and, using their knowledge and understanding, apply the rules to the given situations.

Learners will be aware of registration requirements and the existence of a variety of schemes with different requirements to suit businesses with different needs. They will be able to calculate VAT correctly and use an accounting system to extract the figures required to complete the VAT return.

They will also be aware of special circumstances that require particular attention and be able to deal with errors and changes in the VAT rate, as well as being able to communicate on VAT issues with people inside and outside the business.

Learning outcomes

There are two QCF units involved. Each is divided into component learning outcomes, which in turn comprise a number of assessment criteria.

QCF Unit	Learning Outcome	Assessment Criteria	Covered in Chapter
Preparing and completing VAT returns (skills)	Complete VAT returns accurately and in a timely manner	Correctly identify and extract relevant data for a specific period from the accounting system	**2,3,5-8**
		Calculate accurately relevant inputs and outputs	
		Calculate accurately the VAT due to, or from, the relevant tax authority	
		Make adjustments and declarations for any errors or omissions identified in previous VAT periods	
		Complete accurately and submit a VAT return within the statutory time limits along with any associated payments	
	Communicate VAT information	Inform managers of the impact that the VAT payment may have on the company cash flow and financial forecasts	**7,9**
		Advise relevant people of the impact that any changes in VAT legislation, including the VAT rate, would have on the organisation's recording systems	
		Communicate effectively with the relevant tax authority when seeking guidance	
Principles of VAT (knowledge)	Understand VAT regulations	Identify sources of information on VAT	**1-5,7,8**
		Explain the relationship between the organisation and the relevant government authority	
		Explain the VAT registration requirements	

QCF Unit	Learning Outcome	Assessment Criteria	Covered in Chapter
		Identify the information that must be included on business documentation of VAT-registered businesses	
		Recognise different types of inputs and outputs	
		Identify how different types of supply are classified for VAT purposes	
		Explain the requirements and the frequency of reporting for the following VAT schemes	
		Recognise the implications and penalties for the organisation resulting from failure to abide by VAT regulations including the late submission of VAT returns	

Delivery guidance: Preparing and completing VAT returns

1.   Complete VAT returns accurately and in a timely manner

1.1   Correctly identify and extract relevant data for a specific period from the accounting system

- Learners will be expected to extract relevant net and VAT figures from the accounting system
    - Sales day book
    - Purchases day book
    - Cash book
    - Petty cash book
    - Journal
    - General ledger accounts for sales, purchases, input VAT, output VAT

1.2   Calculate accurately relevant inputs and outputs

- Using the basic rounding rule (rounding down total VAT to the nearest penny) calculate correctly the VAT and input and output figures for
    - Standard supplies
    - Exempt supplies

- – Zero-rated supplies

- – Imports

- – Exports

- – The detailed rounding rules based on lines of goods and services and tax per unit or article are not required

- *No knowledge required of the detail of which specific items fall into each category of standard, exempt and zero-rated.*

- Be able to calculate VAT from net sales amounts at different rates of VAT, including cases when a settlement discount is offered.

- Be able to calculate the amount of VAT arising when given either the gross amount or the net amount of a supply.

- Know in broad terms how imports and exports, and their related VAT, are treated on a VAT return, including the significance of the EC.

- Know that exports are normally zero-rated.

- Correctly account for VAT on business entertainment, sales and purchases of cars and vans and deposits or advance payments.

- Be aware of fuel scale charges and the effect on the total VAT payable/reclaimable (but no calculations).

1.3 Calculate accurately the VAT due to, or from, the relevant tax authority

In respect of

- Transactions in the current period.

- Adjustments for bad debt relief

1.4 Make adjustments and declarations for any errors or omissions identified in previous VAT periods

- The errors or omissions will be given.

- Identify whether the error or omission can be corrected on the current VAT return by identifying the threshold at which errors must be declared and the timescale during which corrections can be made

- Apply the correct treatment.

- How to report an error that cannot be corrected on the current VAT return.

1.5 Complete accurately and submit a VAT return within the statutory time limits along with any associated payments

- Knowledge of what the time limits are, including those relating to non-standard schemes.

- Accurate calculation of the VAT due to, or from, HMRC, both in respect of transactions in the current period and also in relation to errors and omissions identified from previous periods.

- – Transactions include sales and purchase invoices and credits, cash payments and receipts, petty cash payments,

- ■ Complete a VAT return (VAT 100, paper or online version); Boxes 1 to 9.

- ■ Be aware that most businesses will need to submit the VAT return and pay online

- ■ Understand that the balance on the VAT control account should agree to the figure on the VAT return and provide explanations for any difference.

2 Communicate VAT information

2.1 Inform managers of the impact that the VAT payment may have on the company cash flow and financial forecasts

- ■ Know the time limits within which payment must be made under various schemes

- ■ Communicate this via standard communication methods such as emails.

2.2 Advise relevant people of the impact that any changes in VAT legislation, including the VAT rate, would have on the organisation's recording systems

- ■ Basic understanding of the implication of a change in the VAT rate on the organisation using either manual or computerised systems.

- ■ Basic understanding of who would need to be informed and why.

- ■ Advise relevant people by email or other appropriate means.

2.3 Communicate effectively with the relevant tax authority when seeking guidance

- ■ Using letters

Delivery guidance: Principles of VAT

1 Understand VAT regulations

1.1 Identify sources of information on VAT

- ■ Extract information from relevant sources

1.2 Explain the relationship between the organisation and the relevant government authority

- ■ Understanding that

  - – HMRC is a government body entitled to require organisations to comply with VAT regulations in relation to registration, record keeping, submission of returns etc

  - – VAT is a tax on consumer expenditure

  - – It is advisable to get written confirmation from HMRC about issues on which doubt may arise as to the correct treatment

  - – HMRC are entitled to inspect VAT records

1.3 Explain the VAT registration requirements

- The registration threshold and when registration becomes compulsory

- Circumstances in which voluntary registration may be beneficial to the business

- Awareness of circumstances when deregistration may be appropriate, and the de-registration threshold

- Which records must be kept and for how long

1.4 Identify the information that must be included on business documentation of VAT-registered businesses

- And by implication information that is not required

- Including less detailed VAT invoices and VAT receipts, and invoicing for zero-rated and exempt supplies

- Tax points – basic and actual, including where payment is in advance of supply or invoice is after the supply, but not continuous supply. The importance of tax points for determining eligibility for schemes, correct rate of VAT, and including figures on the VAT return.

- Time limits for VAT invoices including the 14-day rule

- Rounding rules

1.5 Recognise different types of inputs and outputs

- What are inputs and outputs, and what are input and output tax?

- How to treat different types of inputs and outputs in preparing a VAT return, including

  - Pro forma invoices

- the implication of the difference between zero-rated and exempt supplies with respect to reclaiming input VAT should be recognised

1.6 Identify how different types of supply are classified for VAT purposes

- Standard supplies

- Exempt supplies

- Zero-rated supplies

- Imports

- Exports

- *No knowledge required of the detail of which specific items fall into each category*

- The basics of partial exemption, including an awareness of the de minimus limit that enables full recovery of input VAT for businesses with mixed exempt and taxable supplies. Calculations will not be required.

1.7 Explain the requirements and the frequency of reporting for the following VAT schemes

- Annual accounting

- Cash accounting

- Flat-rate scheme

- Standard scheme

- Be able to explain in broad terms the way in which each scheme works and the situations in which an organisation would be likely to use one.

- Know the effect of each scheme on the frequency of VAT reporting and payments.

1.8 Recognise the implications and penalties for the organisation resulting from failure to abide by VAT regulations including the late submission of VAT returns

- The main principles of the enforcement regime, but not the fine detail.

    - What triggers a surcharge liability notice. Will not be expected to know how the amount of the surcharge is calculated, or what happens if a further default arises in the surcharge period, etc.

    - Penalties – awareness of fines and that evasion of VAT is a criminal offence

chapter 1:
THE VAT SYSTEM

chapter coverage 📖

Although you will have come across Value Added Tax (VAT) in your earlier studies, we begin this chapter with a reminder of how the VAT system works and then consider some of the more detailed areas you will meet when dealing with and accounting for VAT. The topics covered are:

✍ The value added tax system

✍ HM Revenue and Customs' web site

✍ The VAT Guide

✍ A tax on consumer expenditure

✍ Information that must be kept for VAT purposes

✍ Sales records

✍ Purchases and expenses records

VALUE ADDED TAX – THE SYSTEM

What is VAT?

Value Added Tax (VAT) is essentially a sales tax – it is a tax on spending and is an important source of revenue for the government. Similar forms of sales tax are also charged in many other countries, although you only need to be aware of the system in the UK.

VAT regulation

The VAT system in the UK is administered by HM Revenue & Customs (HMRC), which is the combined body that used to be both the Inland Revenue and HM Customs and Excise (the body responsible for VAT).

In the assessment you will be provided with reference material that will contain the rates and allowances that you will need in the assessment.

Increasingly, HMRC issues advice notes and guidance online via its web site www.hmrc.gov.uk. This is updated far more frequently than the paper publications and you should get used to searching the HMRC web site in preference to relying on hard copy publications.

However, HMRC also issues VAT 700 "The VAT Guide", which provides a business with all the information it needs about accounting for, recording and paying over VAT. The VAT Guide can be sent to you free of charge by simply contacting the National Advice Service (NAS). Alternatively, you can access it at HMRC's web site. You are not expected to know all of the details of The VAT Guide but the main elements will be covered throughout this text.

HMRC does not update The VAT Guide on a regular basis, and it may be necessary to look at the web site for other guidance to ensure that you are looking at the most up-to-date information.

The Business Link website contains some VAT reference material that is kept more up to date and can be found at http://www.businesslink.gov.uk/bdotg/action/layer?r.s=tl&r.l1=1073858808&r.lc=en&topicId=1083126673

Before we begin to look at how the VAT system works we will start with a brief reminder of the details of how a business must record and account for VAT.

Many accountants rely on commercially produced tax tables for details of current rates and allowances. These rates and allowances will be referred to throughout this text.

OPERATION OF VALUE ADDED TAX

If the sales of a business exceed a certain amount for a year then a business must register for VAT. This means that they have a VAT registration number which must be included on invoices and other business documents.

What this also means is that the business must charge its customers VAT on all of its taxable supplies or sales normally at the standard rate of 17.5%. This is known as OUTPUT VAT or OUTPUT TAX (VAT on goods going 'OUT' of the business).

There is, however, a benefit in that the VAT that the business pays when buying from suppliers or paying expenses can be recovered back from HMRC and is known as INPUT VAT or INPUT TAX (VAT on goods coming 'IN' to the business).

Every three months (usually) the business must complete a VAT return (see later chapter) showing the output and input VAT. The business effectively acts as an agent for HMRC. So that

- OUTPUT VAT charged to customers is to be paid over to HMRC, and
- INPUT VAT charged to the business by suppliers is to be reclaimed from HMRC

The excess of output VAT over input VAT must be paid to HMRC with the VAT return. However, if the input VAT exceeds the output VAT then a refund is due from HMRC (this will be dealt with in detail in a later chapter).

HOW IT WORKS

Let's follow a simple manufacturing process through the VAT payment process.

Business	Transaction		HMRC VAT due
Supplier of wood	Sells wood to table manufacturer for £160 + VAT of £28		
	Sale value	£160	
	Output VAT	£28	£28
Table manufacturer	Purchases wood from supplier for £160 + VAT of £28		
	Sells table to retailer for £280 + VAT of £49		
	Sale value	£280	
	Purchases value	£160	
	Output VAT – Input VAT (£49 – £28)	£21	£21

3

Business	Transaction		HMRC VAT due
Retailer	Purchases table from manufacturer for £280 + VAT of £49		
	Sells table to customer for £360 + VAT of £63		
	Sale value	£360	
	Purchases value	£280	
	Output VAT – Input VAT (£63 – £49)	£14	£14
Customer	Purchases table for £360 + VAT of £63		
	Pays retailer (£360 + £63)	£423	£0
Total VAT paid to HMRC			£63

Note that it is the final customer (consumer) – often a member of the general public - who suffers the cost of the VAT. The table cost him £423 not £360, but the customer does not have to pay this to HMRC as this has already been done throughout the chain of manufacture and sale.

Task 1

Business A sells goods to Business B for £1,000 plus £175 of VAT. Which business treats the VAT as input tax and which treats it as output tax?

	Input tax ✓	Output tax ✓
Business A		✓
Business B	✓	

VAT AND ACCOUNTING RECORDS

VAT affects most of the everyday transactions of a business. A VAT-registered business will charge VAT on its sales and will pay VAT on its purchases and expense payments. These sales, purchases and expenses may be on credit or they may be for cash.

The VAT Guide sets out in detail the records that should be kept by a VAT-registered business. Each individual business accounting system will be different but, in general terms, you must keep records of all taxable goods and services which you receive or supply. In practice, you must also be able to distinguish between supplies that are

- standard-rated (17 ½ %)
- reduced rate (5%)
- zero-rated (0%) and
- exempt supplies (no VAT).

However in the assessment you will be told to which category a supply belongs. These will all be considered in more detail in a later chapter.

The records must be kept up-to-date in order that each quarter the correct amount of VAT due to or from HMRC can be calculated and entered onto the VAT return. Whatever method of keeping these records the business uses, they must be kept in such a way that HMRC officers can easily check that the figures on the VAT returns are correct.

Information that must be recorded

The information that must be kept by all businesses in order to be able to correctly calculate the VAT due includes the following:

- Details of all goods or services the business received on which VAT has been charged
- Any services that are received from abroad
- Details of all trade within the European Union
- Details of all supplies made by the business including zero-rated and exempt supplies
- Details of any goods exported

HMRC requires that these records should normally be kept for six years.

HMRC has an entitlement to inspect a taxpayer's VAT records at any time.

Sales records

In order to be able to determine the correct total for the output tax of a business, detailed records of all sales made must be kept.

A SALES INVOICE will be issued to the customer showing the details of the goods or services sold, the amount due, the date the amount is due and any other terms such as discounts. If you send VAT invoices out to customers then copies of these should be kept and the details required can be summarised from them on a quarterly basis. You not only need the invoice totals but also the amounts of the supplies made including zero-rated and exempt supplies.

A CREDIT NOTE is issued to the customer showing the details of the goods returned, the total amount of the goods and the reason for the credit note. Alternatively a customer may send in a DEBIT NOTE with any goods returned. If any credit notes are sent out to customers or debit notes received from customers which alter VAT invoices, copies of these should also be kept.

These detailed records are considered further in the next chapter.

The accounting records that most businesses keep in order to record their sales are the following:

Sales day book – this is a record of all of the invoices sent out to credit customers showing the net amount of the sale, the VAT and the invoice total.

Sales returns day book – this is a record of all of the credit notes sent out to credit customers or debit notes received from credit customers for returns and alterations to invoice amounts. Again, this will show the net amount of the credit/debit note, the VAT and full value of the credit/debit note. Some businesses do not keep a separate sales returns day book; instead the details are recorded in the sales day book with brackets around each of the figures to indicate that they should be deducted.

Cash receipts book – this records receipts from credit customers as well as other receipts for cash sales. You will remember from your accounting studies that the amount to be recorded for the receipts from credit customers is the full invoice total – the VAT does not need to be analysed here as this has already been done in the sales day book. However, where cash sales are made and VAT has been charged on the sale then the cash receipts book should show the net amount of the sale, the VAT and the final total.

Purchases and expenses records

When a business receives invoices for purchases or expenses then these must all be kept. The business must keep PURCHASE INVOICES for goods and services received that are not only standard-rated but also zero-rated and reduced rate supplies. They must be kept and filed in such a way that they can be easily produced for HMRC, if necessary. You can only claim input VAT if you have a valid VAT invoice.

There is an exception for the requirement for a valid VAT invoice in order to reclaim input tax. For the following types of expenditure, if the total is £25 or less including VAT then no invoice is required:

- Telephone calls from public or private telephones

- Purchases through coin operated machines

- Car park charges (although on-street parking meters are not subject to VAT)

As well as keeping the VAT invoices the business must also keep detailed records of all taxable supplies including any zero-rated supplies. This will normally be done in the following accounting records.

Purchases day book – this is a record of all of the invoices received from credit suppliers showing the net amount of the supply, the VAT and the invoice total.

Purchases returns day book – this is a record of all of the credit notes received by the business and any debit notes issued. Again, these will be analysed to show the net amount of the credit, any VAT and the total of the credit/debit note. Some businesses do not keep a separate purchases returns day book. Instead the details of any credit/debit notes are shown in the purchases day book with each figure in brackets to indicate that it should be deducted from the invoice totals.

Cash payments book – this is a record of all of the payments made by the business. The payments to credit suppliers are recorded as the total payment with no analysis of the VAT element as this has already been analysed out in the purchases day book. However, all other payments for goods or expenses that have attracted VAT should be recorded as the net amount, the VAT and the full amount of the payment.

It is important to note that not only must all sales, purchases and expenses be recorded in the accounting records, but copies of all documentation, sales invoices and purchases/expenses invoices, credit notes and debit notes must also all be kept.

Task 2

On which ONE of the following can input tax be reclaimed without a valid invoice?

	✓
Telephone calls from home phone of £28 (including VAT)	
Purchases of snacks costing £10 (including VAT) from a shop for a business meeting	
Multi storey car parking charges of £21 (including VAT)	✓
Purchases of pens and pencils using petty cash of £18 (including VAT)	

Petty cash records

When a business makes minor payments, for example small items of office stationery, or purchases of tea and coffee for staff, money is taken out of the petty cash box. This is evidenced by a PETTY CASH VOUCHER. The petty cash voucher must be retained by the business and contains details of the expense incurred and any VAT charged. It is usual for the purchase invoice to be attached to the petty cash voucher. You can only claim the input VAT if you have the valid VAT invoice, and not just the petty cash voucher.

Petty cash payments book – this is a record of all of the payments made by the business. Details of petty cash vouchers will be recorded in the PETTY CASH PAYMENTS BOOK.

The journal

The JOURNAL is the book of prime entry for non-standard transactions such as payroll transactions, writing off bad debts and correcting errors, that do not fall into any of the day books mentioned above. Some of the journal entries may have an impact on VAT such as the writing off of a bad debt relating to a standard rated supply.

CHAPTER OVERVIEW

- The VAT system is administered by HM Revenue and Customs, which issues VAT 700 "The VAT Guide" and various other advice notes and guidance via its web site

- The ultimate consumer bears the cost of the VAT

- All VAT-registered persons must keep full records of the details of goods and services the business received on which VAT has been charged, any services received from abroad, details of all trade within the European Union, details of all supplies made by the business including zero-rated and exempt supplies and details of any goods exported

- These records should normally be kept for six years and must be made available to an HMRC officer if required

- Copies of sales invoices must be kept and the main accounting records for sales will be the sales day book, sales returns day book and cash receipts book

- All invoices for purchases and expenses must be kept otherwise the input VAT cannot be reclaimed – the main accounting records for purchases and expenses are the purchases day book, the purchases returns day book and the cash payments book

Keywords

Output VAT or Output tax – VAT on the sale of goods and the provision of services. This is paid by the business to HMRC

Input VAT or Input tax – VAT on the purchases of goods and payment of expenses. This is reclaimed by the business from HMRC, provided there is a valid VAT invoice.

TEST YOUR LEARNING

Test 1

Which organisation administers VAT in the UK? Tick the relevant box below.

	✓
HM Customs and Excise	
Inland Revenue	
HM Revenue and Customs	✓
HM Treasury	

Test 2

Choose which ONE of the following statements is correct. Tick the relevant box below.

	✓
Output VAT is the VAT charged by a supplier on the sales that are made by his business. Output VAT is collected by the supplier and paid over to HMRC.	✓
Output VAT is the VAT suffered by the purchaser of the goods which will be reclaimed from HMRC if the purchaser is VAT registered and a valid VAT invoice is held.	

Test 3

Explain how it is that the final consumer pays the full amount of VAT to the seller but never pays any money to HMRC.

Test 4

How long does HMRC usually require relevant documents to be kept? Tick the relevant box below.

	✓
1 year	
2 years	
6 years	✓
20 years	

Test 5

A business has not kept either suppliers' invoices received, or copies of sales invoices sent out. Tick the relevant boxes below.

	True ✓	False ✓
Copies of sales invoices do not need to be kept		✓
Supplier invoices must be kept as evidence of input VAT incurred	✓	

chapter 2:
ACCOUNTING FOR VAT

───────────── **chapter coverage** 📖 ─────────────

In this chapter we begin to look at the detailed VAT requirements, specifically focusing on the detail to be included in various types of VAT invoice, and how the detail of the books and records comes onto the VAT control account. The topics covered are:

✍ VAT invoices

✍ VAT control account

VAT INVOICES

If a business is registered for VAT and it sends out an invoice to another VAT-registered business then it must send a VAT invoice within 30 days of the supply as shown below:

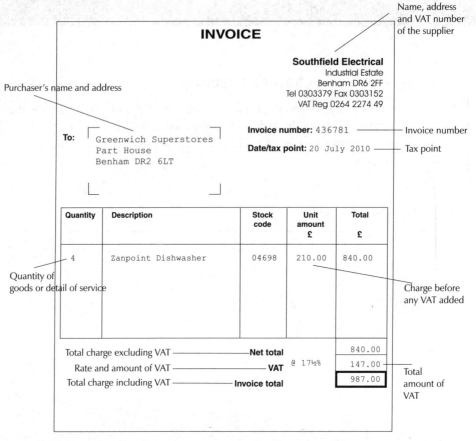

The issuing of a sales invoice by a business,

- increases the output VAT, and so

- increases the amount payable to HMRC by the business.

The receipt of a purchase invoice by a VAT registered business,

- increases the input VAT, and so

- increases the amount to be reclaimed from HMRC by the business.

We now consider some of the details of this VAT invoice further.

Type of supply

The following types of supply must be identified separately on a VAT invoice:

- Sale
- Hire purchase or conditional sale
- Loan
- Exchange
- Hire, lease or rental
- Process (making goods from someone else's materials)
- Sale on commission, for example by an auctioneer
- Sale or return

Task 1

Which three of the following items must be included on a valid VAT invoice?

- Customer VAT registration number
- Supplier VAT registration number ✓
- Total VAT exclusive amount ✓
- Total VAT amount ✓
- Total VAT inclusive amount

Foreign currency invoices

If a VAT invoice is issued in a foreign currency then the VAT must be calculated on the amounts expressed in sterling. The foreign currency amounts should be converted using the UK market selling rate as published in national newspapers or a period rate of exchange published by HMRC.

Less detailed VAT invoice

If a business is in the retail trade then the customer should always be given a VAT invoice if so requested by the customer.

However, if the charge for the goods is less than £250, including VAT, then a LESS DETAILED VAT INVOICE can be issued showing:

- Business name, address and VAT registration number

- The time of supply

- A description of the goods or services supplied

- For each VAT rate applicable, the total amount payable including the VAT and the VAT rate charged.

In particular, note that no details relating to the customer, or VAT exclusive amounts are required.

Modified invoice

If the amount charged for the goods or services exceeds £250, and the customer requests a VAT invoice a full VAT invoice or, if the customer agrees, a MODIFIED INVOICE must be supplied.

The amounts that must be shown on a modified invoice are the VAT inclusive amount of each standard-rated or reduced rate supply rather than the net of VAT amount.

At the bottom of the modified invoice the following must be shown separately:

- Total VAT inclusive amount of the standard-rated or reduced rate supplies
- Total VAT payable on those supplies
- Total value, net of VAT, of the supplies
- Total value of any zero-rated supplies included on the invoice
- Total value of any exempt supplies included on the invoice

The modified invoice must also show all of the other factors included on a full VAT invoice such as the tax point and VAT registration number.

Pro forma invoice

A PRO FORMA INVOICE is often used in order to offer goods to a potential customer at a certain price and to invite the customer to send a payment in return for which the goods will be dispatched. This is often the case when a business does not wish to sell on credit but instead needs payment up front before the goods are dispatched.

When the pro forma invoice is received by the potential customer it cannot be used by the customer as evidence to reclaim the VAT element. Therefore any pro forma invoice should be clearly marked "THIS IS NOT A VAT INVOICE".

If the customer does decide to buy the goods or sends payment then a proper VAT invoice must be issued. The customer can only reclaim input tax when they receive a proper VAT invoice.

Task 2

A purchase invoice for taxable supplies has just been processes. What will be the effect on VAT? Choose ONE answer.

	✓
Input tax will increase	✓
Input tax will decrease	
Output tax will increase	
Output tax will decrease	

CREDIT NOTES AND DEBIT NOTES

If a customer returns goods then it is customary to issue a CREDIT NOTE to reflect the value of these goods, including the VAT element. Alternatively, the customer may, if both parties agree, issue a DEBIT NOTE which reflects the value of the goods returned and the VAT element. Credit notes and debit notes can also be issued to correct errors that have been made on the original invoice.

The issuing of a sales credit note by a business,

- decreases the output VAT, and so

- decreases the amount payable to HMRC by the business.

The receipt of a purchase credit note by a VAT registered business,

- decreases the input VAT, and so

- decreases the amount to be reclaimed from HMRC by the business.

To be a valid credit or debit note for VAT purposes the following must occur:

- The credit/debit note must reflect a genuine mistake or change in value of the goods supplied and must be issued within one month of the mistake or alteration being discovered or agreed

- It must be headed clearly as a credit note or debit note

- It must include the same type of information as an standard VAT invoice plus additionally:

  - The reason for the issue

  - The number and date of the original VAT invoice

- Any zero-rated or exempt supplies can be included on the credit/debit note but must be totalled separately and it must show clearly that there is no VAT on these items

Replacement of returned goods

If a customer returns goods and these are replaced with similar goods there are two options:

- Allow the original VAT invoice to stand – therefore there is no need to account for VAT on the replacement goods; or

- Cancel the original VAT invoice by issuing a credit note – then charge VAT on the replacement goods with a new invoice.

If the replacement goods are supplied at a different price to the original goods, there are again two options:

- If the replacement goods are at a lower price than the originals then the VAT charge can be reduced by issuing a credit note

- If the replacement goods are issued at a higher price than the original goods then the additional VAT must be accounted for by issuing a further invoice for the additional amount

THE VAT CONTROL ACCOUNT

The central record that is used to record the overall VAT position and complete the VAT return, is the VAT ACCOUNT, or as it is often called in a business's ledger, the VAT CONTROL ACCOUNT. Here all of the entries from the accounting records such as the sales and purchases day books are entered and the amount of tax due to HMRC for the quarter or due to be reclaimed is calculated.

HOW IT WORKS

Given below is a typical VAT control account set out in the manner suggested in The VAT Guide.

VAT CONTROL ACCOUNT

VAT deductible – input tax	£	VAT payable – output tax	£
VAT on purchases – from the purchases day book	3,578.90	*VAT on sales – from the sales day book*	5,368.70
VAT on purchases – from the cash payments book	586.73	*VAT on sales – from the cash receipts book*	884.56
Sub-total	4,165.63	**Sub-total**	6,253.26
Less:		Less:	
VAT on credit notes from suppliers – purchases returns day book	–49.70	*VAT on credit notes to customers – sales returns day book*	–69.80
Total tax deductible	4,115.93	**Total tax payable**	6183.46
		Less: total tax deductible	–4,115.93
		Payable to HMRC	2,067.53

The entries shown above are explained below. In later chapters we will return to the VAT control account to add more entries.

VAT deductible

- The VAT on credit purchases is taken from the VAT column of the purchases day book and the VAT on cash purchases is taken from the VAT column of the cash payments book and petty cash payments book – these totals should be posted regularly from the day books to the VAT control account, usually on a weekly or a monthly basis

- The deduction for VAT on credit notes and debit notes is taken from the VAT column total of the purchases returns day book. If credit notes are recorded in the purchases day book then the VAT on them must be totalled and not included in the earlier total for the purchases day book

VAT payable

- The VAT on credit sales is taken from the VAT column of the sales day book and the VAT on cash sales is taken from the VAT column of the cash receipts book – these totals should be posted regularly from the day books to the VAT control account usually on a weekly or monthly basis

- The deduction for VAT on credit notes to customers is taken from the VAT column of the sales returns day book. If credit notes are recorded in the sales day book instead, then the total of VAT on these credit notes will have to be calculated and not included when posting the total of the sales day book VAT earlier in the VAT control account

Tax payable

- The total tax payable less the total tax deductible gives the amount that is due to HMRC for the period ie if there is an excess of output VAT, tax is payable to HMRC.

- If the total tax payable is less than the total tax deductible, the difference is the amount that can be reclaimed from HMRC for the period ie if there is an excess of input VAT, tax is reclaimable/ recoverable from HMRC.

CHAPTER OVERVIEW

- If goods are supplied for less than £250, including VAT, a less detailed VAT invoice can be issued which shows only the VAT inclusive amount and the rate of VAT – however if the customer asks for a full VAT invoice, this must be supplied

- If the amount charged for the goods exceeds £250 and the customer agrees, a modified VAT invoice can be issued – this shows the net, VAT and gross amounts of the supplies in total

- If a pro forma invoice is sent out to a potential customer this must be clearly marked "This is not a VAT invoice" as the customer cannot use it to reclaim any input VAT

- The central accounting record for recording VAT is the VAT control account which lists all of the VAT deductible, or input tax, on the debit side and all of the VAT payable, output tax, on the credit side – the balance on this account is the amount of VAT due to or from HMRC for the period

Keywords

VAT invoice – an invoice that allows input VAT to be claimed or output VAT to be charged

VAT control account or VAT account – the ledger account in which all amounts of input tax and output tax are recorded

TEST YOUR LEARNING

Test 1

Which TWO of the following statements about pro forma invoices are correct? Tick the relevant boxes below.

	✓
A pro forma invoice is always sent out when goods are sent to customers, before issuing the proper invoice	
A pro forma invoice always includes the words 'This is not a VAT invoice'	✓
A customer can reclaim VAT stated on a pro forma invoice	
A pro forma invoice is sent out to offer a customer the chance to purchase the goods detailed	✓

Test 2

Given below is information about the VAT of a business that has been taken from the books of prime entry:

	£
VAT figures	
From the sales day book	9,147.96
From the sales returns day book	994.67
From the purchases day book	6,344.03
From the purchases returns day book	663.57
From the cash receipts book	1,662.78
From the cash payments book	936.58

You are to write-up the VAT control account.

VAT CONTROL ACCOUNT

VAT deductible	£	VAT payable	£
	6344.03		9147.96
	936.58		1662.78
	7280.61		10810.74
−	663.57		− 994.67
Total VAT deductible	6617.04	Total VAT payable	9816.07
			6617.04
			3199.03

Picklist:

- Sales day book
- Sales returns day book
- Purchases day book
- Purchases returns day book
- Cash receipts book
- Cash payments book
- Less VAT deductible
- Less VAT payable
- Due to HMRC
- Reclaimed from HMRC

chapter 3:
TYPES OF SUPPLY

chapter coverage 📖

The VAT treatment of a supply depends on whether VAT needs to be charged and, if so, at which rate. There are special rules that apply when goods and services enter and exit the UK. The topics covered are:

✍ Types of supply

✍ Rates of VAT

✍ Imports and exports

TYPES OF SUPPLY

Supplies of goods or services fall into one of three categories:

- Outside the scope of VAT
- Exempt supplies
- Taxable supplies

Outside the scope of VAT

Supplies outside the scope of VAT have no effect for VAT.

These include paying wages or dividends.

Exempt supplies

EXEMPT SUPPLIES are supplies on which no VAT is charged at all, at any rate. The details of exempt supplies are found in section 29 of The VAT Guide. Examples of exempt supplies are:

- Post Office postal services
- Education
- Healthcare
- Insurance
- Betting and gambling

If a supplier only sells exempt supplies then he cannot register for VAT (see later) and so cannot reclaim the input VAT on any of his purchases and expenses. For example, an insurance company cannot reclaim the VAT on its expenses as its supplies (selling insurance) are exempt. So the cost to the insurance company of its purchases and expenses is the VAT inclusive amount.

You are not required to know which specific items are treated as exempt supplies for the assessment.

TAXABLE SUPPLIES

There are three rates of VAT in the UK:

- Standard rate 17.5%
- Reduced rate 5%
- Zero rate 0%

A trader making taxable supplies can register for VAT. Once registered, the trader must therefore charge VAT on his supplies at the relevant rate, but as a result can reclaim input VAT on his purchases and expenses.

Standard-rated supplies

The vast majority of supplies of goods and services are STANDARD-RATED SUPPLIES. A supply should be treated as standard-rated, ie charging VAT at 17½%, unless it specifically fits into one of the other categories.

Reduced-rated supplies

A reduced rate of VAT (5%) applies to certain supplies such as domestic fuel and power. Think of these supplies as standard rated supplies (but special rules apply to allow 5% VAT to be charged on them).

Zero-rated supplies

ZERO-RATED SUPPLIES are supplies of goods and services which are technically taxable but the law states that the rate of VAT on these goods is 0%. The main reason for this is that these zero-rated supplies are normally essential items which, if they were taxed, would be an additional burden to the less well-off.

As with exempt supplies the details of supplies that are zero-rated are set out in section 29 of The VAT Guide.

Examples of zero-rated supplies are:

- Young children's clothes and shoes
- Most food purchased in shops (but not in restaurants)
- Bus and train fares
- Books
- Newspapers and magazines

The effect on a business which sells zero-rated supplies is that although it charges output VAT at 0% on its sales it is allowed to VAT register and so can reclaim any input VAT on its purchases. Therefore a bus company charges no VAT on its fares but it is able to reclaim from HMRC any VAT on its purchases and expenses such as fuel and service costs. So the cost to the bus company of its purchases and expenses is the VAT exclusive amount.

The difference between exempt supplies and zero-rated supplies is that if a supplier sells exempt supplies then he cannot reclaim the input VAT on any of his purchases and expenses.

You are not required to know which specific items are treated as zero rated supplies for the assessment.

Task 1

The following businesses have just paid telephone bills of £1,175 (£1,000 plus VAT of £175).

What is the net cost incurred by each business in relation to the telephone bills?

Business type	Type of supply made	Net cost £
Insurance company	Only exempt supplies	1175
Accountancy firm	Only standard rated supplies	1000
Bus company	Only zero rated supplies	1000

IMPORTS AND EXPORTS

The treatment of VAT on purchases from other countries and sales to other countries depends upon whether the purchase or sale is from, or to, another country within the European Union (EU) or outside it. The treatment also differs depending upon whether the purchase/sale is of goods or of services.

We look at each situation in turn.

Goods purchased from outside the EU

If goods are brought into the United Kingdom from a country that is not part of the EU this is known as an "import" and the following treatment is required for VAT:

- The VAT is normally deemed to be at the same rate as on a supply of the same goods in the UK. This VAT is usually paid by the customer to HMRC as the goods enter the UK (ie at the docks or the airport)

- The VAT paid at the docks/ airport is then reclaimed as input tax on the VAT return

The net effect is the same as buying from a UK supplier:

- Buying from a UK supplier, the customer pays the VAT to the supplier (as part of the invoice total), then reclaims the input VAT from HMRC on the VAT return

- Buying from outside the EU, the customer pays the VAT to HMRC at the port or airport, then reclaims the input VAT from HMRC on the VAT return

3: Types of supply

Goods acquired from inside the EU

Goods that are purchased from another country within the EU are known as ACQUISITIONS rather than imports. If goods are purchased by a UK buyer from a VAT-registered business in another EU country, and the goods are sent to the UK, the EU supplier will not charge VAT (neither will HMRC at the ports/airports).

Instead, the UK purchaser must charge himself the VAT due on those goods on his VAT return. This VAT can be treated as input tax as well as being an amount of output tax due to HMRC.

Again the net effect is the same as above BUT no cash changes hands

- Buying from a supplier in another EU country the customer 'pays' output tax to HMRC on the VAT return, then 'reclaims' the input VAT from HMRC on the VAT return (net effect nil)

Services received from outside the UK

If a business receives certain services from outside the UK then for VAT purposes the services are treated as though the business has supplied them and the VAT on them is treated as output tax. Their value counts towards the business's taxable turnover.

The services for which this is the appropriate treatment are listed in section 31 of The VAT Guide and include the following:

- Advertising services
- Transfer of copyright, patents, licenses, trademarks etc
- Services of consultants, engineers, lawyers, accountants etc
- Banking, financial and insurance services

Goods exported

Goods exported to any country outside the EU are normally treated as zero-rated supplies provided that there is documentary evidence of the export and that this is obtained by the supplier within three months of the supply.

Goods sold to an EU customer are known as a "dispatch". There are two different scenarios:

- If the EU customer is a **VAT-registered business** in the EU country he will be charged VAT at the ZERO rate. To benefit from zero rating, he must provide his **EU VAT-registration number** (which is then shown on the invoice). Additionally the VAT registration numbers of both the supplier and customer must include the EU country code (for example GB).

- If the customer is **not EU VAT registered** (or his EU VAT registration number has not been given) then UK VAT is charged as if a normal UK sale (ie STANDARD rate in most cases).

Services exported

Some supplies of services to customers overseas are zero-rated while others are standard-rated. Details of the VAT rate on services can be found in section 29 of The VAT Guide.

Supplies of goods within the EU

Any UK VAT-registered business which makes supplies of goods to traders registered for VAT in another EU country must complete a sales list showing the value of these supplies of goods. This is done on Form VAT 101 normally on a quarterly basis and sent to HMRC.

Task 2

A UK trader sells goods to both registered and non-registered traders elsewhere in the EU. If these goods had been sold in the UK they would have been standard-rated. Which of the following is the correct treatment assuming all other conditions are fulfilled? Tick the relevant box.

To registered traders	To non-registered traders	✓
Zero-rated	Zero-rated	
Standard-rated	Zero-rated	
Zero-rated	Standard-rated	✓
Standard-rated	Standard-rated	

HOW IT WORKS

The VAT control account from the previous chapter is shown again below. Some additional items shown in italics are explained below.

VAT CONTROL ACCOUNT

VAT deductible – input tax	£	VAT payable – output tax	£
VAT on purchases – from the purchases day book	3,578.90	VAT on sales – from the sales day book	5,368.70
VAT on purchases – from the cash payments book	586.73	VAT on sales – from the cash receipts book	884.56
	4,165.63		6,253.26
VAT allowable on EU acquisitions	211.78	*VAT due on EU acquisitions*	211.78
Sub-total	4,377.41	**Sub-total**	6,465.04
Less:		Less:	
VAT on credit notes from suppliers – purchases returns day book	–49.70	VAT on credit notes to customers – sales returns day book	–69.80
Total tax deductible	4,327.71	**Total tax payable**	6,395.24
		Less: total tax deductible	–4,327.71
		Payable to HMRC	2,067.53

VAT deductible and payable

- The VAT on acquisitions from other European Union countries is shown as both input tax and output tax as the VAT must be paid on the acquisition but can also be deducted as allowable input tax

EU statistics

The value of the supply or acquisition of goods from other EU countries must be shown on the VAT return (see later chapter). This information is used to provide statistics on movements of taxable goods within the EU.

CHAPTER OVERVIEW

- In the UK there are three rates of VAT – the standard rate of 17.5%, a reduced rate of 5% for certain supplies such as domestic fuel and power and the zero rate. There are other goods and services which are entirely exempt from VAT

- There is no VAT charged on either zero-rated supplies or exempt supplies – however if a business makes exempt supplies it cannot reclaim the input tax on its purchases and expenses – if the supplies made by the business are zero-rated then input VAT can be reclaimed

- Goods imported from outside the EU are normally deemed to be charged at the same rate as goods in the UK

- Services received from outside the EU are treated as if the business has supplied them and the output tax must be included on the VAT return

- The VAT on acquisitions of goods from other EU countries is treated as both output tax and input tax

- Exports of goods to another country outside the EU are normally treated as zero-rated supplies – services supplied to a customer in another country may be either zero-rated or standard-rated

- If a business makes sales of goods within the EU, a sales list must be completed quarterly and sent to HMRC

Keywords

Supplies outside the scope of VAT – supplies which have no effect for VAT purposes (salaries and dividends)

Standard-rated supplies – goods and services which are taxable at a rate of 17½ %

Reduced-rated supplies – goods and services which are taxable at a rate of 5%

Zero-rated supplies – goods and services which are taxable but the rate of tax on them is 0%

Exempt supplies – supplies on which no VAT is charged

Acquisitions – goods purchased from another European Union country

Dispatches – goods sold to another European Union country

TEST YOUR LEARNING

Test 1

Input numbers where indicated below.

The three rates of VAT in the UK are:

17·5	%
5	%
0	%

Test 2

Identify whether the following statements are true or false.

	True ✓	False ✓
If a business supplies zero rated services then the business is not able to reclaim the VAT on its purchases and expenses from HMRC.		✓
A business makes zero rated supplies. The cost to the business of its purchases and expenses is the VAT exclusive amount.	✓	

Test 3

A UK VAT-registered business is exporting goods which are standard-rated in the UK to an American business. Which ONE of the following statements is correct? Tick the relevant box.

	✓
The goods will be treated as standard rated in the UK if the American business is VAT registered	
The goods will be treated as standard rated in the UK provided documentary evidence of the export is obtained within 3 months	
The goods will be treated as zero rated in the UK if the American business is VAT registered	
The goods will be treated as zero rated in the UK provided documentary evidence of the export is obtained within 3 months	✓

chapter 4:
VAT REGISTRATION AND DEREGISTRATION

chapter coverage 📖

During the life of a business there may be times when the person making supplies may want to register for VAT or may be required to VAT register. Similarly, there could be situations where that person wants to deregister or must deregister. The topics covered are:

✍ Registration for VAT

✍ VAT deregistration

REGISTRATION FOR VAT

It has already been mentioned that a business must register for VAT if its turnover exceeds the registration limit, which from April 2009 is £68,000. However the situation is slightly more complicated than that. There are two situations in which a business must register for VAT, as set out below

Historic turnover rule

When, at the end of a month (the relevant month),

(a)   the TAXABLE TURNOVER, the value of a business's taxable supplies, for the prior period (but not looking back more than twelve months) has exceeded the registration limit, £68,000, then

(b)   the business must apply within 30 days of the end of that period to register, and

(c)   it will be registered from one month and one day after the end of the relevant month (ie VAT must be charged on taxable supplies).

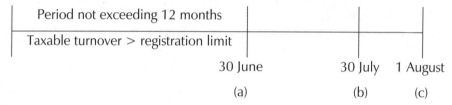

Period not exceeding 12 months		
Taxable turnover > registration limit		
30 June	30 July	1 August
(a)	(b)	(c)

HOW IT WORKS

Jack started in business on 1 July 2009. His monthly VAT exclusive turnover is:

	£
Standard rated supplies	5,000
Zero rated supplies	1,850
Exempt supplies	600
TOTAL	7,450

Step 1   Calculate the VAT exclusive TAXABLE turnover for each month (standard plus reduced plus zero-rated supplies). Exclude both sales of capital assets and exempt supplies.

Taxable turnover is £6,850 per month (£5,000 + £1,850)

Step 2   Work out when the £68,000 registration limit is exceeded (if at all), up to a maximum of a 12 month period.

After 9 months (31 March 2010) cumulative turnover is £61,650, so the limit is not exceeded.

After 10 months (30 April 2010) cumulative turnover is £68,500, so the limit is exceeded.

Step 3   Work out the date by which HM Revenue and Customs must be notified (30 days after the end of the relevant month.)

HMRC must be notified by 30 May 2010 (30 April plus 30 days)

Step 4   Work out the date of registration ie the date from which VAT must be charged (end of the relevant month plus 1 month and one day)

Jack is VAT registered from 1 June 2010 (30 April plus 1 month and 1 day).

Future turnover rule

When, at any time,

(a)   the taxable turnover (before any VAT is added) is expected to exceed the annual registration limit within the next 30 days alone, then

(b)   again the business must apply within 30 days to be registered for VAT, but

(c)   it is registered from the beginning of the 30-day period

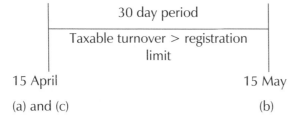

HOW IT WORKS

Orla has been in business for many years with VAT exclusive turnover of approximately £5,500 per month (£66,000 per annum).On 24 November 2009 Orla won a major contract which will immediately bring in additional income of approximately £65,000 per month.

Step 1   Work out whether Orla's business will exceed the registration threshold of £68,000 in the next 30 days alone.

Taxable turnover in the next 30 days is £70,500 (£5,500 + £65,000), which exceeds the threshold.

Step 2   Work out the date by which HM Revenue and Customs must be notified (30 days after the date when we become aware the threshold will be exceeded.)

HMRC must be notified by 24 December 2009 (24 November plus 30 days)

Step 3   Work out the date of registration ie the date from which VAT must be charged (the date on which we become aware that the threshold will be exceeded)

Orla is VAT registered from 24 November 2009 (ie immediately).

A business must be extremely careful to ensure that if either its current turnover for the prior period or its expected turnover within the next 30 days will exceed the registration limit then it must apply to register for VAT.

If a business does not apply to register within the 30-day limit in these circumstances, then it is liable to a fine. In addition, if HMRC discovers in the future that the business should have been registered, but wasn't, the business may have to

- repay all output VAT that should have been charged if it had registered but

- not be allowed to reclaim any input VAT.

These rules apply to suppliers of both standard-rated and zero-rated goods and services.

New and growing businesses that are not VAT registered are therefore recommended to monitor their cumulative turnover on a monthly basis.

In order to register for VAT the business must complete Form VAT 1 which is available to download from the HMRC website. The business can also apply online through the HMRC website.

Once registered for VAT you are known as a REGISTERED PERSON.

Task 1

Amy started trading on 1 August 2008. Her monthly sales (excluding VAT) are:

	£
Standard-rated supplies	6,850
Zero-rated supplies	1,070
Exempt supplies	700
	8,820

8120

By what date must Amy apply to HMRC be registered for VAT?

- 30 April 2009
- 1 May 2009
- 30 May 2009 ✓
- 1 June 2009

Voluntary registration

If a business's taxable turnover is below the annual registration limit it is still possible for the business to register for VAT on a voluntary basis. Why might a business do this?

The main advantage of voluntary registration is the ability to recovery input tax.

In particular, if a business makes zero-rated supplies then it may be advantageous to register for VAT.

- output VAT at 0% (ie nil) has to be charged on its sales but
- it can reclaim the input VAT on its purchases and expenses.

Therefore the business is in a net cash repayment position.

Some businesses may want to VAT register to project the image of the business. However the disadvantages include:

- the administrative burden of preparing regular VAT returns,
- the potential for incurring penalties, and
- loss of business from non registered customers if prices increase by output tax

Registration decision tree

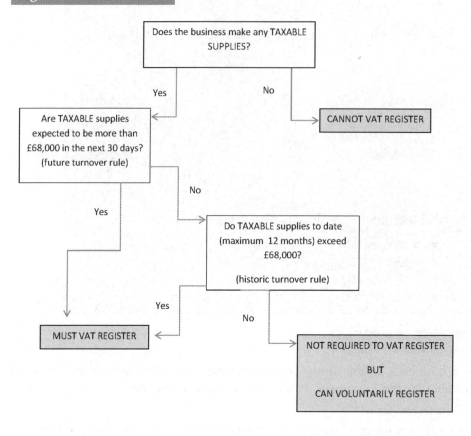

DEREGISTRATION

Deregistration is compulsory if a person ceases to make taxable supplies and has no further intention of making taxable supplies.

The person must notify HMRC within 30 days. Deregistration will take effect on the date taxable supplies ceased.

Voluntary deregistration

A VAT-registered business may find that its taxable turnover either falls or is expected to fall. If the taxable turnover for the next twelve months is expected to fall beneath the deregistration limit, which from April 2009 is £66,000, then the business can apply to HMRC to deregister.   68.000

CHAPTER OVERVIEW

- When a business's taxable turnover reaches the registration limit then the business must register for VAT within 30 days otherwise the business is liable to be fined

- Some businesses may find it advantageous to register for VAT although the registration limit has not been met – this is known as voluntary registration

- If a business stops making taxable supplies, and does not intend to make them in the future then the business must deregister

- If a business's taxable turnover falls below the deregistration limit then the business can apply to HMRC to deregister

Keywords

Registration – VAT must be charged on taxable supplies from the date of registration

Deregistration – VAT cannot be charged on any supplies from the date of deregistration

TEST YOUR LEARNING

Test 1

You have been contacted by a potential new client, Mrs Quirke. She has recently started trading as an interior designer. Complete the following letter to her explaining when her business must register for VAT.

AN Accountant
Number Street
London
SW11 8AB

Mrs Quirke
Alphabet Street
London
W12 6WM

Dear Mrs Quirke
VAT REGISTRATION

Further to our recent telephone conversation, set out below are the circumstances when you must register your business for VAT.

If the taxable turnover of your business for the prior period, but not looking back more than [12] months, has exceeded the registration limit of £ [70,000] then the business must apply to register within [30 DAYS] of the end of that period. It will be registered from [1 MONTH 1 DAY] after the end of the relevant month.

Alternatively, if at any time, the taxable turnover (before any VAT is added) is expected to exceed the annual registration limit within the next [30 DAYS], then the business must apply within [30 DAYS] to be registered for VAT, but is registered from [start 30 days]. This would be the situation if, for example, you obtained a large one-off contract for, say, £70,000.

If you wish to discuss this in any more detail please do not hesitate to contact me.

Yours sincerely

AN Accountant

chapter 5:
OUTPUT TAX AND INPUT TAX

CALCULATION OF VAT

VAT charged on taxable supplies is based on the VAT exclusive value. For standard-rated supplies this is at 17.5%.

Sometimes the VAT inclusive price is given, for example on less detailed VAT invoices. On such an invoice the actual amount of VAT charged is not shown separately. In order to calculate the amount of VAT included in this invoice the VAT fraction of 17.5/117.5 or 7/47 must be used.

Similarly you may need to calculate the VAT for reduced-rated supplies. The VAT fraction to be applied to VAT inclusive totals is 5/105 or 1/21.

HOW IT WORKS

An invoice shows a total VAT inclusive amount of £47.00. The amount of VAT at 17.5% included in this amount can be calculated in one of two ways:

$$£47.00 \times 17.5/117.5 = £7.00$$

or

$$£47.00 \times 7/47 = £7.00$$

Another invoice for a reduced-rated supply shows a total VAT inclusive amount of £42.00. The VAT included in this amount can be calculated as

$$£42.00 \times 5/105 = £2.00$$

or

$$£42.00 \times 1/21 = £2.00$$

Task 1

Complete the following table.

VAT exclusive	VAT rate	VAT	VAT inclusive
£	%	£	£
	17.5		51.11
	5		18.90

Rounding of VAT

VAT is calculated on the cost of the goods or services.

When VAT is calculated for individual lines on an invoice, the calculation can be rounded in either of two ways.

- Round down to the nearest 0.1p (so 86.76p would be 86.7p); or
- Round to the nearest 0.5p, so 86.7p would be 87p.

The total VAT on an invoice should be rounded to the nearest 1p.

The normal treatment would be to round down and this is the method to be applied in the assessment.

OUTPUT TAX

Tax point

You will note the date/TAX POINT on the invoice. This is an important date as it is the date on which the sale was made for the purposes of the VAT return.

When goods are supplied, the BASIC TAX POINT is normally the date on which the goods are either taken away by the customer or sent to the customer.

When services are provided, the basic tax point is normally the date on which the service was provided.

The basic tax point is over-ridden if there is an ACTUAL TAX POINT.

An actual tax point is created if:

- The invoice is issued before the basic tax point or
- Payment is received before the basic tax point.

Then the date of invoice or the payment is the actual tax point, depending upon which happens first.

If this earlier tax point above does not apply and if the issue of the VAT invoice is up to 14 days after the basic tax point, then the invoice date is the actual tax point.

This 14-day rule may be varied provided that the HMRC National Advice Service is contacted. For example an extension of the 14-day rule may be required if invoices are usually issued on a monthly basis.

If a VAT invoice is issued more than 14 days after the basic tax point without approval to extend the 14-day rule, the tax will be due at the basic tax point, ie the date on which the goods or services were supplied.

HOW IT WORKS

To identify the relevant tax point of a transaction you need to go through the following steps:

Step 1   Identify the following three dates,

BASIC TAX POINT (delivery or collection date)

Invoice date

Payment date

Step 2   Work out which of these is the earliest date.

Step 3   Follow the decision tree:

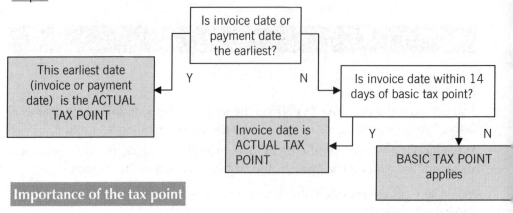

Importance of the tax point

The importance of the tax point, whether it is the basic tax point or the actual tax point, is that

- The rate of VAT is fixed by the tax point, particularly important where there is a change in the rate of VAT and;

- The output tax must be paid over to HMRC at the end of the period which covers this tax point.

Task 2

A business sends goods out to a customer on 15 May 2009. The VAT invoice is then sent later and is dated 20 May 2009. The customer paid the invoice on 20 June 2009. What is the tax point for these goods?

	✓
15 May 2009	
20 May 2009	✓
20 June 2009	

Pro forma invoices

Sometimes suppliers send out pro forma invoices. These have no relevance for tax point. The tax point is determined based on the date of the real invoice.

Deposits

Sometimes customers pay a deposit in advance. If a deposit is paid, there will be separate tax points for the deposit and the balancing payment.

HOW IT WORKS

On 1 August a customer sent in a 15% deposit with an order. The goods were sent out to the customer on 6 August, and an invoice issued on 25 August. The customer paid the remaining 85% on 30 September.

The tax point for the deposit is determined by looking at:

- The basic tax point (delivery date)   6 August
- The invoice date,   25 August
- The deposit payment date   1 August

Actual tax point is created as deposit is paid before the basic tax point.

Tax point is 1 August (actual tax point)

The tax point relating to payment of the balance is determined by looking at:

- The basic tax point (delivery date)   6 August
- The invoice date   25 August
- The date of payment of the balance   30 September

The basic tax point is the earliest date so no actual tax point is created. Also the invoice date is more than 14 days after the basic tax point, so invoice date can be ignored.

Tax point is 6 August (basic tax point)

Task 3

A business received an order, with a 10% deposit from a customer on 2 June 2009. The goods were sent out to the customer on 11 June 2009. The VAT invoice for the full amount is dated 29 June 2009. The customer paid the remaining 90% on 31 July 2009. Identify ONE or TWO tax point(s) for these goods?

	✓
2 June 2009	✓
11 June 2009	✓
29 June 2009	
31 July 2009	

Cash or settlement discounts

If a cash or settlement discount is offered to a customer, VAT is always calculated on the basis that the customer will take advantage of the discount. If the customer does not in fact take the settlement discount but pays the invoice in full there is no requirement to charge any additional VAT. The VAT that is charged and shown on the invoice is the amount that should be accounted for on the VAT return.

HOW IT WORKS

Goods are supplied to a customer with a total VAT exclusive list price of £800.00. The customer is allowed a 10% trade discount and is also offered an additional 3% settlement discount.

The VAT would be calculated as follows:

	£
List price	800.00
Less: trade discount	80.00
Net price	720.00
Less: settlement discount	21.60
	698.40
VAT £698.40 × 17.5%	122.22
On the invoice you would see:	
VAT exclusive	720.00
VAT@17.5%	122.22
Invoice total	842.22

The customer could pay £842.22, or (£842.22 – £21.60) = £820.62 if the terms for the receiving cash discount are complied with. In either case, no adjustment is made to the amount of output tax.

Task 4

A business sells goods to a customer for £1,000. The customer is allowed a 20% trade discount and is offered a 2% settlement discount for payment within 14 days. If the goods are standard-rated how much VAT would be charged on them, assuming that the customer does not pay within the 14 day period?

	✓
£175.00	
£171.50	
£140.00	
£137.20	✓

VAT AND BAD DEBTS

If goods or services are supplied on credit the VAT will have been accounted for when the original VAT invoice was issued. If the debt is never paid by the customer and is written-off as bad in the accounting records, BAD DEBT RELIEF is available. Bad debt relief means that it is possible to reclaim the VAT that will have been paid to HMRC on that supply provided that certain conditions are met, most importantly that:

- The debt must be more than six months overdue (note this is measured from the date when the payment was due)
- The VAT must have been paid to HMRC
- The debt must be written-off in the business's accounts

The VAT on the bad debt is shown on the VAT control account as an INCREASE IN THE INPUT VAT to be reclaimed.

HOW IT WORKS

A bad debt arises, for example, when a customer has not paid after a long period of time or when a customer goes into liquidation.

Step 1   An entry is made into the journal book to ensure that the bad debt is reflected in the accounting records.

	Debit £	Credit £
Bad debts expense account (VAT exclusive amount)	100.00	
VAT control account (INPUT VAT)	**17.50**	
Sales ledger control account (VAT inclusive amount)		117.50

Step 2   When a period of more than 6 months since due payment date has passed, bad debt relief can be claimed. THERE IS AN INCREASE IN INPUT VAT recoverable.

Task 5

What effect will claiming VAT bad debt relief have on the amount of VAT due to HMRC? Choose ONE answer.

	✓
The amount payable will increase	
The amount payable will decrease	✓

FUEL SCALE CHARGES

Where a business purchases fuel for cars and retains a VAT invoice it can reclaim the input VAT on that fuel. This input VAT will simply be part of the input VAT within the totals from the purchases day book or the cash payments book.

However, the fuel provided by the business to the owner or an employee may be used partly for private motoring. An amount of output tax is charged at a scale rate to take account of this private fuel. The fuel scale charge is based solely on the carbon dioxide rating of the car. The scale charge will increase the amount payable to HMRC.

HOW IT WORKS

An employee has a car provided by the business. The business purchases all petrol for the car and the employee uses the car for both business and private purposes.

Within the purchases day book or petty cash payments book are VAT invoices for petrol. As a result, the input tax on these is reclaimed from HM Revenue and Customs each accounting period as the VAT is included within the totals on those day books, ie the business is also reclaiming VAT on private fuel.

To offset against this the journal book will include an entry for a scale charge in relation to the private fuel used by the employee.

If for example the car has emissions such that the specified scale charge is £28.15, the journal book will include an entry

	Debit £	Credit £
Motor expenses account	28.15	
VAT control account (OUTPUT VAT)		**28.15**

The OUTPUT VAT will increase.

VANS

When there is private use of a van and fuel is provided any of the following three arrangements can be put in place.

- The input VAT can be apportioned to reflect the business: private use of the fuel,

- Output VAT can be declared on charges at least equal to the cost of the fuel used for private purposes, with full deduction of input VAT on the purchase of fuel, and

- The scale charge system can be used, with deduction of input VAT on the purchase of fuel

These provisions to not need to be applied where the private use of the van is on a small scale and incidental to the main use of the van, for example where the van goes to the employee's house overnight for security of the vehicle.

HOW IT WORKS

The VAT control account from the earlier chapter is shown again below. Additional items shown in italics are explained below.

VAT CONTROL ACCOUNT

VAT deductible – input tax	£	VAT payable – output tax	£
VAT on purchases – from the purchases day book	3,578.90	VAT on sales – from the sales day book	5,368.70
VAT on purchases – from the cash payments book	586.73	VAT on sales – from the cash receipts book	884.56
	4,165.63		6,253.26
VAT allowable on EU acquisitions	211.78	VAT due on EU acquisitions	211.78
Bad debt relief	33.60	*Fuel scale charge*	28.15
Sub-total	4,411.01	**Sub-total**	6,493.19
Less:		Less:	
VAT on credit notes from suppliers – purchases returns day book	–49.70	VAT on credit notes to customers – sales returns day book	–69.80
Total tax deductible	4,361.31	**Total tax payable**	6,423.39
		Less: total tax deductible	–4,361.31
		Payable to HMRC	2,062.08

These entries will now be explained.

VAT deductible

- The bad debt relief is a claim for repayment of VAT already paid to HMRC on a sale to a customer who has never paid. The debt is over six months old and the bad debt has been written-off in the accounting records. It is shown as INPUT VAT on the VAT return/ VAT control account.

VAT payable

- The fuel scale charge is a payment corresponding to the element of private fuel consumption where VAT has been reclaimed on all fuel purchased by a business. It is shown as OUTPUT VAT on the VAT return/ VAT control account.

INPUT TAX

Irrecoverable input tax

Although we have said that businesses can reclaim VAT on purchases and expenses there are some items of expenditure on which VAT cannot be reclaimed from HMRC. The main examples of this are:

- Business entertainment expenses. However input VAT on entertaining staff is recoverable.

- Cars purchased (eg company cars for sales people etc), including fitted accessories and delivery charges, unless the car is used exclusively for business purposes (eg pool car). Note that VAT is recoverable on the purchase of a van.

Usually the cost to a VAT registered business of buying goods and services is the VAT exclusive amount.

	£
Amount paid to supplier (VAT inclusive)	1,175
Input VAT reclaimed from HMRC	(175)
Net cost to the business (VAT exclusive)	1,000

However where VAT is irrecoverable (entertaining or cars) the cost to the business is the VAT inclusive amount.

Partial exemption

A taxable person may only recover the VAT paid on supplies to that person so far as it is attributable to taxable supplies made by that person. Where a trader makes a mixture of taxable and exempt supplies (for example a dentist – dental services are exempt, but selling toothbrushes and toothpaste is taxable), there may be **partial exemption**. Where a trader is partially exempt, not all input VAT is recoverable because some of it is attributable to exempt supplies made by that person.

A partially exempt business has the problem of trying to analyse the input tax suffered into two categories.

- **Attributable to making taxable supplies** (buying toothbrushes) – (fully recoverable)

- **Attributable to making exempt supplies** (buying dentistry consumables) – (not recoverable unless very small)

HMRC may agree various methods with a trader to allow this apportionment to be calculated. The most popular method used is called the **standard method**, which involves the following steps.

<u>Step 1</u>   Calculate the amount of input VAT suffered on supplies made to the taxable person in the period.

<u>Step 2</u>   Calculate how much of the input VAT suffered relates to supplies which are wholly used or to be used by him in making taxable supplies. This input VAT is deductible in full.

<u>Step 3</u>   Calculate how much of the input VAT suffered relates to supplies which are wholly used or to be used by him in making exempt supplies. This input VAT is not deductible.

<u>Step 4</u>   Calculate how much of any remaining input VAT is deductible. This is calculated using a percentage. The percentage is (taxable turnover excluding VAT/total turnover excluding VAT) × 100%. For all but very large businesses this percentage is rounded up to the next whole percentage above.

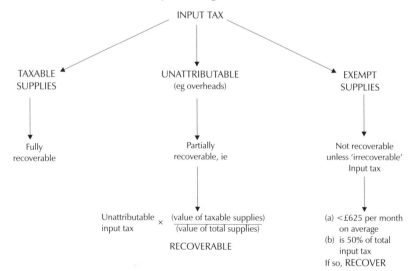

You do not need to calculate the recoverable v exempt input tax for your assessment but must be aware of how it works and the 'de minimis' limits.

If the exempt input tax is small it can also be reclaimed. To be 'small' two conditions must each be met.

- The input VAT wholly attributable to exempt supplies plus the VAT apportioned to exempt supplies is no more than £625 a month on average

- The exempt input tax is also no more than 50% of all input VAT

This limit is known as the ***de minimis* limit**.

HOW IT WORKS

The businesses shown below all make a mixture of exempt and taxable supplies.

	VAT on exempt supplies	Exempt input tax small?	Exempt input tax proportion	Exempt input tax small?
Business A	£500 per month on average	✓	40% of total input tax	✓
Business B	£600 per month on average	✓	55% of total input tax	x
Business C	£650 per month on average	x	45% of total input tax	✓

Business A – as exempt input tax is small using both tests ALL input tax can be reclaimed

Businesses B and C – only fulfil the criteria for one of the small tests, therefore only input VAT relating to taxable supplies (ie buying toothbrushes above) can be reclaimed.

CHAPTER OVERVIEW

- The basic tax point is the date on which goods are sent to a customer or services are provided for a customer. This basic tax point can be over-ridden by the actual tax point – the actual tax point can be created if an invoice is issued or a payment received before the goods or services are sent out or by sending out an invoice after the supply of the goods providing that this is within 14 days of the supply

- VAT is calculated on the cost of the goods or services after deduction of any trade discount – if a settlement discount is offered the VAT is calculated on the invoice amount less the discount – VAT is always rounded down to the nearest penny

- If a business writes-off a bad debt that is more than six months old and the output VAT on the supply has already been paid to HMRC, this VAT can be reclaimed from HMRC

- The VAT on business entertainment expenses and the purchase of cars for use within a business is non-reclaimable

- If a VAT-registered business makes both taxable and exempt supplies the recovery of input tax will be restricted subject to the *de minimis* limits

Keywords

Tax point – the date which determines when the VAT must be accounted for to HMRC

Basic tax point – the date on which goods are delivered or services provided

Actual tax point – a further date that can override the basic tax point if certain conditions are met

Bad debt relief – a reclaim of output VAT when a written off debt is more than 6 months overdue

Fuel scale charge – an output VAT charge to offset against the input VAT reclaimed on fuel purchased for private use

Partial exemption – when a business makes a mixture of taxable and exempt supplies then only part of the input VAT may be reclaimed subject to the de minimis limits

TEST YOUR LEARNING

Test 1

Business C sells goods to Business D for £384.00 plus the standard rate of VAT. Both businesses are VAT registered.

(a)

The VAT is £	

(b) Which business will treat it as output tax and which will treat it as input tax?

	Output tax ✓	Input tax ✓
Business C	✓	
Business D		✓

Test 2

Identify which two of the following purchases have irrecoverable input tax

	✓
Diaries for staff	
Car for sales manager	✓
Photocopier	
Entertaining clients	✓

Test 3

In each of the following situations state the tax point and whether this is a basic tax point or an actual tax point (B or A):

	Date	Basic/ Actual
An invoice is sent out to a customer for goods on 22 June 2009 and the goods are dispatched on 29 June 2009	22	
Goods are sent out to a customer on 18 June 2009 and this is followed by an invoice on 23 June 2009	23	
A customer pays in full for goods on 27 June 2009 and they are then delivered to the customer on 2 July 2009.	27	

Test 4

For each of the following situations calculate the amount of standard rated VAT that would appear on the invoice:

	£
A VAT exclusive list price of £356.79 will have VAT of	
A VAT exclusive list price of £269.00 where a trade discount of 15 % is given will have VAT of	
A VAT exclusive list price of £250.00 where a 2.5% settlement discount is offered will have VAT of	
A VAT exclusive list price of £300.00 where a trade discount of 10% is given and a 3% settlement discount is offered will have VAT of	

Test 5

You have received four invoices from suppliers which show only the total VAT inclusive price and the fact that all of the goods are standard-rated. For each invoice total determine the amount of VAT that is included.

Complete the following table.

VAT inclusive £	VAT at 17 ½ % £
42.88	
96.35	
28.20	
81.07	

Test 6

State three conditions for the VAT on a bad debt to be reclaimed from HMRC?

chapter 6:
VAT RETURN

chapter coverage 📖

So far we have considered the detailed rules for determining the correct amount of VAT. In this chapter we look at how all of this is reported to HMRC on the VAT return. The topics covered are:

✍ The VAT return

✍ The VAT control account

✍ The VAT return online

THE VAT RETURN

A VAT RETURN, Form VAT 100, will normally need to be completed for each three-month accounting period, known as the tax period. When a business registers for VAT it will be allocated to one of three groups of tax periods.

Group 1 – tax periods ending on the last day of March, June, September and December

Group 2 – tax periods ending on the last day of April, July, October and January

Group 3 – tax periods ending on the last day of May, August, November and February

A business can apply to have a tax period that fits in with its financial year.

Completing the VAT return

Towards the end of each tax period a business will receive notice that a VAT return is due. The paper form sent out by HMRC is called Form VAT 100. The return must be completed and then submitted to the VAT Central Unit , arriving no later than ONE MONTH after the end of the tax period.

The VAT return should be completed in ink and all boxes should be completed, writing "none" if necessary.

It is also possible to submit the VAT return online using the HMRC web site.

Boxes 1 to 9, the number entry boxes, of the VAT return are shown on the next page.

All newly registered VAT traders and all those with sales over £100,000 (excluding VAT), must file their VAT returns online and pay electronically from April 2010.

Where the VAT return is submitted online, the taxpayer has an additional seven calendar days for the return to reach HMRC.

A VAT Notice 700/12 Filling in Your VAT Return is available from the VAT National Advice Service or the HMRC web site, and can help in completing the return.

VAT due in this period on **sales** and other outputs (Box 1)

VAT due in this period on **acquisitions** from other **EC Member States** (Box 2)

Total VAT due **(the sum of boxes 1 and 2)** (Box 3)

VAT reclaimed in the period on **purchases** and other inputs, including acquisitions from the EC (Box 4)

Net VAT to be paid to HM Revenue & Customs or reclaimed by you **(Difference between boxes 3 and 4)** (Box 5)

Total value of **sales** and all other outputs excluding any VAT. **Include your box 8 figure** (Box 6)

Whole pounds only

Total value of purchases and all other inputs excluding any VAT. **Include your box 9 figure** (Box 7)

Whole pounds only

Total value of all **supplies** of goods and related costs, excluding any VAT, to other **EC Member States** (Box 8)

Whole pounds only

Total value of all **acquisitions** of goods and related costs, excluding any VAT, from other **EC Member States** (Box 9)

Whole pounds only

The boxes are completed as follows:

Box 1 The total of the VAT on sales, less the VAT on any credit notes issued, together with any adjustments for earlier period errors not exceeding the greater of £10,000 or 1% of turnover (subject to an overall £50,000 limit) – see later chapter.

Box 2 The VAT due on any acquisitions from other European Union countries.

Box 3 The total of boxes 1 and 2.

Box 4 The total of the VAT on purchases and expenses being reclaimed less the VAT on any credit notes received. This total also includes the VAT on any acquisitions from other EU countries and any adjustments for errors on previous VAT returns not exceeding £10,000 or 1% of turnover (subject to a £50,000 limit) – see later chapter.

Box 5   Deduct the figure in box 4 from the figure in box 3 and enter in box 5. If the figure in box 3 is larger than that in box 4 then this total is the amount due to HMRC. If the figure in box 3 is less than the figure in box 4 then the total is the amount that is due from HMRC.

Box 6   The total of all sales less credit notes. This total is excluding VAT but should include the net amount of sales that are standard-rated, zero-rated and exempt as well as any supplies to EU member countries.

Box 7   The total of all purchases and other expenses – less any credit notes. Again, this figure should be the total excluding any VAT and should include standard-rated, zero-rated and exempt supplies. This total should also include any acquisitions from EU member countries.

Box 8   Fill in box 8 with the total value, excluding VAT of all supplies of goods and services to other EU member countries.

Box 9   Fill in box 9 with the total of all acquisitions of goods and related services, excluding VAT, from EU member countries. (Related services includes items such as freight costs and insurance for the goods)

If a payment is due to HMRC then tick the relevant box at the bottom of the form.

Check that all of the figures and arithmetic are correct. Any errors should be crossed out and the correct figures inserted – any amendments should be initialled.

Finally, the form should be checked and authorised by the appropriate senior management figure in the organisation and should then be sent off in the envelope provided together with a cheque, unless payment is made electronically. Ensure that the form is received by VAT Central Unit by the due date and always keep a copy for your own records.

HOW IT WORKS

We will now use the VAT control account from an earlier chapter to illustrate how to complete the VAT return for the period. In accordance with the guidance received from AAT, a standard rate of 17.5% has been used throughout.

VAT ACCOUNT

VAT deductible – input tax	£	VAT payable – output tax	£
VAT on purchases – from the purchases day book	3,578.90	VAT on sales – from the sales day book	5,368.70
VAT on purchases – from the cash payments books		VAT on sales – from the cash receipts book	
(530.79 + 55.94)	586.73		884.56
	4,165.63		6,253.26
VAT allowable on EU acquisitions	211.78	VAT due on EU acquisitions	211.78
Bad debt relief	33.60	Fuel scale charge	28.15
Sub-total	4,411.01	**Sub-total**	6,493.19
Less:		Less:	
VAT on credit notes from suppliers – purchases returns day book	–49.70	VAT on credit notes to customers – sales returns day book	–69.80
Total tax deductible	4,361.31	**Total tax payable**	6,423.39
		Less: total tax deductible	–4,361.31
		Payable to HMRC	2,062.08

Not all of the information for the VAT return is found in the VAT control account so the various day books will need to be consulted as well. These are given below.

Sales day book summary (all UK)

	Zero-rated sales	Standard-rated sales	VAT	Total
	£	£	£	£
Jan 20XX	592.21	11,250.10	1,968.77	13,811.08
Feb 20XX	1,123.79	9,274.55	1,623.05	12,021.39
Mar 20XX	1,865.67	10,153.63	1,776.88	13,796.18
Total	3,581.67	30,678.28	5,368.70	39,628.65

Purchases day book summary

	Zero-rated purchases £	UK purchases Standard-rated purchases £	VAT on UK purchases £	EU purchases £	Total £
Jan 20XX	823.10	7,854.15	1,374.47	421.10	10,472.82
Feb 20XX	1,295.50	8,456.25	1,479.84	392.54	11,624.13
Mar 20XX	551.20	4,140.45	724.59	396.54	5,812.78
Total	2,669.80	20,450.85	3,578.90	1,210.18	27,909.73

Sales returns day book summary

	Zero-rated sales £	Standard-rated sales £	VAT £	Total £
Jan 20XX	5.21	120.10	21.02	146.33
Feb 20XX	10.45	137.25	24.02	171.72
Mar 20XX	9.93	141.51	24.76	176.20
Total	25.59	398.86	69.80	494.25

Purchases returns day book summary (all UK)

	Zero-rated purchases £	Standard-rated purchases £	VAT £	Total £
Jan 20XX	15.89	50.00	8.75	74.64
Feb 20XX	-	56.00	9.80	65.80
Mar 20XX	-	178.00	31.15	209.15
Total	15.89	284.00	49.70	349.59

Cash receipts book summary

	Net £	VAT £	Total £
Jan 20XX	1,234.40	216.02	1,450.42
Feb 20XX	1,867.34	326.78	2,194.12
Mar 20XX	1,952.89	341.76	2,294.65
Cash sales total	5,054.63	884.56	5,939.19

Cash payments book summary

	Net £	VAT £	Total £
Jan 20XX	824.45	144.28	968.73
Feb 20XX	956.76	167.43	1,124.19
Mar 20XX	1,251.84	219.08	1,470.92
Cash purchases	3,033.05	530.79	3,563.84

Petty cash payments book summary

	Net £	VAT £	Total £
Jan 20XX	121.21	21.21	142.42
Feb 20XX	98.15	17.18	115.33
Mar 20XX	100.34	17.55	117.89
Cash purchases	319.70	55.94	375.64

Journal book (extract)

	Debit £	Credit £
Sales	192.00	
VAT control account	33.60	
Sales ledger control account		225.60
The write off of a bad debt (more than 6 months overdue)		
Motor expenses	28.15	
VAT control account		28.15
Fuel scale charge for petrol on car provided for employee		

There were no sales to other countries but the value of the acquisitions from EU countries as shown in the purchases day book was £1,210.18 plus VAT.

The business also had a bad debt and provided petrol for business and private use for an employee's car. The details of these are shown in the extract from the journal book above.

The business's name and address is Far Flung Creations, Zebra House, Horniman Street, Belsing, BE4 6TP. The VAT return is for the tax period ending 30 June 2009 and the business's VAT registration number is 382 6109 14.

How to complete the VAT return

The return is for the first period in 20XX ie to 31 March 20XX.

Now to complete the boxes.

			£
Box 1	VAT on sales from the sales day book		5,368.70
	VAT on sales from the cash receipts book		884.56
	VAT on fuel scale charge		28.15
	Less: VAT on credit notes		(69.80)
			6,211.61
Box 2	EU acquisitions		211.78
Box 3	Total of box 1 and box 2 £6,211.61 + £211.78		6,423.39
Box 4	VAT on purchases from purchases day book		3,578.90
	VAT on purchases from cash payments book		530.79
	VAT on purchases from petty cash payments book		55.94
	VAT on EU purchases		211.78
	Bad debt relief		33.60
	Less: VAT on credit notes from suppliers		(49.70)
			4,361.31
Box 5	Net VAT due Box 3 minus box 4		
	£6,423.39-£4,361.31		2,062.08

Boxes 6 to 9 deal with sales and purchases before any VAT is added. Note that for these boxes no pence are needed.

Box 6	Zero-rated credit sales		3,581
	Standard-rated credit sales		30,678
	Cash sales		5,054
	Less: zero-rated credit notes		(25)
	standard-rated credit notes		(398)
			38,890
Box 7	Zero-rated credit purchases		2,669
	Standard-rated credit purchases		20,450
	Cash purchases		3,033
	Petty cash purchases		319
	EU acquisitions		1,210
	Less: zero-rated credit notes		(15)
	standard-rated credit notes		(284)
			27,382
Box 8	EU sales from sales day book		"none"
Box 9	EU acquisitions from purchases day book		1,210

Finally, the payment box on the return should be ticked as a payment for the amount of VAT due must be sent with the VAT return. Then the VAT return must be checked thoroughly including all calculations and passed to a senior member of management for the declaration to be signed.

VAT due in this period on **sales** and other outputs (Box 1) | 6,211.61

VAT due in this period on **acquisitions** from other **EC Member States** (Box 2) | 211.78

Total VAT due (**the sum of boxes 1 and 2**) (Box 3) | 6,423.39

VAT reclaimed in the period on **purchases** and other inputs, including acquisitions from the EC (Box 4) | 4,361.31

Net VAT to be paid to HM Revenue & Customs or reclaimed by you (**Difference between boxes 3 and 4**) (Box 5) | 2,062.08

Total value of **sales** and all other outputs excluding any VAT. **Include your box 8 figure** (Box 6) | 38,890
Whole pounds only

Total value of purchases and all other inputs excluding any VAT. **Include your box 9 figure** (Box 7) | 27,382
Whole pounds only

Total value of all **supplies** of goods and related costs, excluding any VAT, to other **EC Member States** (Box 8) | None
Whole pounds only

Total value of all **acquisitions** of goods and related costs, excluding any VAT, from other **EC Member States** (Box 9) | 1,210
Whole pounds only

Task 1

Identify which one of the following statements in relation to acquisitions from other EU countries and how they are dealt with on the VAT return is correct?

	✓
Input tax paid at the ports is reclaimed as input tax on the VAT return	
They are shown as both input tax and output tax on the VAT return	
They are zero rated and so do not feature on the VAT return	
They are exempt and so do not feature on the VAT return	

Clearing the VAT account

When the amount of tax due to HMRC is paid then the double entry will be to credit the bank account and debit the VAT account, thereby clearing the account of any balance before the postings for the next period take place – this is illustrated below:

VAT ACCOUNT

VAT deductible – input tax	£	VAT payable – output tax	£
VAT on purchases – from the purchases day book	3,578.90	VAT on sales – from the sales day book	5,368.70
VAT on purchases – from the cash payments books		VAT on sales – from the cash receipts book	
(530.79 + 55.94)	586.73		884.56
	4,165.63		6,253.26
VAT allowable on EU acquisitions	211.78	VAT due on EU acquisitions	211.78
Bad debt relief	33.60	Fuel scale charge	28.15
Sub-total	4,411.01	**Sub-total**	6,493.19
Less:		Less:	
VAT on credit notes from suppliers – purchases returns day book	−49.70	VAT on credit notes to customers – sales returns day book	−69.80
Total tax deductible	4,361.31	**Total tax payable**	6,423.39
		Less: total tax deductible	−4,361.31
Cash paid	2,062.08	**Payable to HMRC**	2,062.08

VAT AND THE EFFECT ON CASH FLOW

The VAT payment must be made with the return no later than ONE MONTH after the end of the tax period. If, however, the payment is made electronically the taxpayer has an additional seven calendar days after the due date for the return to make the payment.

Where the VAT return is submitted online, the taxpayer must pay electronically and therefore has an additional seven calendar days for the payment to reach HMRC. Where the return is submitted online and the VAT paid by direct debit, it will usually be collected a further three days after the additional seven days.

VAT can be a substantial payment for a business to make. Provision should therefore be made to ensure that cash is reserved to pay the VAT after each period.

The person responsible for preparing the VAT return must set timescales for information to be provided to them on a timely basis and to ensure that they have sufficient time to prepare the return before the deadline. Once the return details have been finalised they must contact the person responsible for paying the VAT to ensure that payment is made by the due date.

Task 2

Using the details from the example above complete the email below.

To: Finance Director
From: Accounting Technician
Date: 25 April 20XX
Subject: VAT return to 31 March 20XX

Please be advised that I have now completed the VAT return for the quarter to 31 March 20XX. If you are in agreement with the figures shown in the return please could you arrange an electronic payment of
£ [   ] (number)
to be made by [   ] (date)

If you wish to discuss this further please feel free to call me.

Kind regards

THE VAT RETURN ONLINE

The online VAT return is very similar in appearance to the paper return. However, some of the boxes are completed automatically, for example box 3 is completed automatically, as the addition of boxes 1 and 2.

Once the relevant boxes have been completed there is the opportunity to review the return prior to pressing the 'submit' button. It is also possible to save a partially complete return which is useful if you need to get someone to review the actual return before you press 'submit'. Pressing 'submit' has the same effect as signing the declaration at the bottom of the paper return.

Once submitted the taxpayer is able to print a copy of the return and to obtain a submission reference number. Completed VAT returns for your business will be viewable by you on the HMRC website for 15 months.

Submit a return

VAT period
Period: 04 09
Date from:
　　　01 Aug 2009
Date to:
　　　31 Oct 2009
Due date:
　　　07 Dec 2009 ⓘ

Business details
VAT Registration Number:
　　　382 6109 14
Business name:
　　　FAR FLUNG CREATIONS
Business address:
　　　ZEBRA HOUSE
　　　HORNIMAN STREET
　　　BELSING
　　　BE4 6TP

Enter VAT return figures ⓘ

Please enter the information in the boxes below and click 'Next' to proceed.

* indicates required information

Please note: Enter values in pounds sterling, including pence, for example 1000.00.

Important note

Your 'Total VAT due (Box 3)' and 'Net VAT to be paid to HM Revenue & Customs or reclaimed by you (Box 5)' figures will be calculated automatically when you click 'Next'. The figures will then be displayed on the next screen.

Before entering the figures please follow the link Filling in your VAT Return (opens in a new window)

VAT due in this period on **sales** and other outputs (Box 1):

VAT due in this period on **acquisitions** from other **EC Member States** (Box 2):

Total VAT due **(the sum of boxes 1 and 2)** (Box 3):　　　**Calculated value**

VAT reclaimed in this period on **purchases** and other inputs, (including acquisitions from the EC)
(Box 4):

Net VAT to be paid to HM Revenue & Customs or reclaimed by you **(Difference between boxes 3 and 4)** (Box 5):　　　**Calculated value**

Total value of **sales** and all other outputs excluding any VAT. **Include your box 8 figure** (Box 6):

Whole pounds only
(If you use the Flat Rate scheme, in this box please enter the amount **including** VAT, not **excluding** VAT. See Public Notice 733 (opens in a new window) for further information).

Total value of **purchases** and all other inputs excluding any VAT. **Include your box 9 figure** (Box 7):

Whole pounds only
Total value of all **supplies** of goods and related costs, excluding any VAT, to other **EC Member States**

(Box 8)
Whole pounds only
Total value of all **acquisitions** of goods and related costs, excluding any VAT, from other **EC Member**

States (Box 9):
Whole pounds only

Next　Back

70

CHAPTER OVERVIEW

- Normally every quarter the VAT return, Form VAT 100 must be completed and submitted to HMRC together with any payment due within one month of the end of the tax period

- The first five boxes of the VAT return can be completed from the figures in the VAT control account

- Boxes 6 to 9 must be completed from the other accounting records of the business showing sales and purchases, exports and acquisitions excluding VAT

Keywords

VAT return – Form VAT 100 which must normally be completed to show the amount of VAT due or to be reclaimed for the quarter

VAT Central Unit – the central VAT office that sends out the VAT returns and to whom the completed VAT return and any payment due must be sent

TEST YOUR LEARNING

Test 1

Given below are extracts from the books of prime entry for the business: Martin Trading, Blackness House, Jude Street, Clinford, CL3 6GH. The business's VAT registration number is 225 3756 12 and the tax period is March to June 2009. In accordance with the guidance received from AAT, a standard rate of 17.5% has been used throughout.

Sales day book summary

	Zero-rated sales £	Standard-rated sales £	VAT £	Total £
Total	13,447.67	45,267.44	7,921.80	66,636.91

Purchases day book summary

	Zero-rated purchases £	Standard-rated purchases £	VAT £	Total £
Total	7,447.30	30,627.58	5,359.82	43,434.70

Sales returns day book summary

	Zero-rated sales £	Standard- rated sales £	VAT £	Total £
Total	225.83	773.56	135.37	1,134.76

Purchases returns day book summary

	Zero-rated purchases £	Standard-rated purchases £	VAT £	Total £
Total	215.61	714.20	124.98	1,054.79

Cash receipts book summary

	Net £	VAT £	Total £
Cash sales	5,054.63	884.56	5,939.19

Cash payments book summary

	Net £	VAT £	Total £
Cash purchases	3,352.75	586.73	3,939.48

As well as the purchases shown in the purchases day book there were also acquisitions from EU countries totalling £2,256.07 plus £394.81 of VAT.

You are required to complete boxes 1 to 9 of the VAT return given.

VAT due in this period on **sales** and other outputs (Box 1)

VAT due in this period on **acquisitions** from other **EC Member States** (Box 2)

Total VAT due **(the sum of boxes 1 and 2)** (Box 3)

VAT reclaimed in the period on **purchases** and other inputs, including acquisitions from the EC (Box 4)

Net VAT to be paid to HM Revenue & Customs or reclaimed by you **(Difference between boxes 3 and 4)** (Box 5)

Total value of **sales** and all other outputs excluding any VAT. **Include your box 8 figure** (Box 6)

Whole pounds only

Total value of purchases and all other inputs excluding any VAT. **Include your box 9 figure** (Box 7)

Whole pounds only

Total value of all **supplies** of goods and related costs, excluding any VAT, to other **EC Member States** (Box 8)

Whole pounds only

Total value of all **acquisitions** of goods and related costs, excluding any VAT, from other **EC Member States** (Box 9)

Whole pounds only

chapter 7:
SCHEMES FOR SMALL BUSINESSES

chapter coverage 📖

Over many years it has been recognised that VAT has become a burden that is especially tough for small businesses. Several schemes have been devised in order to help small businesses. The topics covered are:

✍ Annual accounting

✍ Cash accounting

✍ Flat rate scheme

SPECIAL SCHEMES

There are a number of special schemes which make VAT accounting easier for small businesses.

Annual accounting scheme

The ANNUAL ACCOUNTING SCHEME is helpful to small businesses as it cuts down the administrative burden of VAT by allowing the business to submit one VAT return every 12 months. The VAT return is due within two months of the end of the year.

Under this scheme the business makes nine (usually) equal monthly direct debit payments of 1/10 of the estimated of the amount of VAT liability for the year. If the business has been trading for a period of time, the estimate will usually be the liability of the previous 12 months. The first payment is due at the end of the fourth month.

The balancing payment will be sent with the VAT return, within two months after the year end.

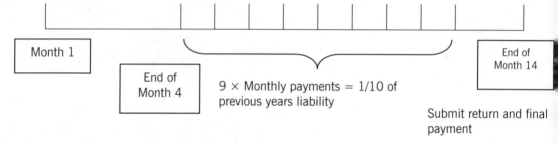

Use of this annual accounting scheme is a great help to a small trader as it means that he does not have to prepare a quarterly VAT return. However, it does mean that he must still keep accurate accounting records of the VAT information for a whole year.

The limits for joining and leaving this scheme are:

	VAT exclusive taxable turnover £
Join the scheme if turnover in the next 12 months is expected to be below (exclude capital supplies)	1,350,000
Leave the scheme if turnover in the previous 12 months exceeds	1,600,000

Full details of the annual accounting scheme can be found in VAT Notice 732 (August 2009) VAT: Annual Accounting.

Task 1

A trader has joined the annual accounting scheme for the year ended 31 December 2010. Identify whether the following statement is true or false. (Insert a tick)

	True	False
The first payment due to HMRC is by 1 April 2010.		

Cash accounting scheme

Provided a business has a clean record with HMRC, it may be able to apply to use the CASH ACCOUNTING SCHEME. All VAT returns and payments must be up-to-date and the business must not have been convicted of a VAT offence or penalty in the previous 12 months.

The scheme allows the accounting for VAT to be based upon the date of receipt or payment of money rather than the tax point on an invoice.

This is particularly useful for a business which gives its customers a long period of credit but has to pay its suppliers promptly as under the cash accounting scheme

- OUTPUT VAT will be paid to HMRC later as cash is received later from customers, but

- INPUT VAT is reclaimed at the same time/ earlier as suppliers are paid early.

The opposite is also true, this is unhelpful for a business which receives a long period of credit from its suppliers but receives payment promptly from its customers as under the cash accounting scheme

- OUTPUT VAT will be paid to HMRC at the same time/ earlier as cash is received early from customers, but

- INPUT VAT is reclaimed at the later as suppliers are paid later.

The scheme also gives automatic relief from bad debts since no output VAT is payable to HMRC if the customer does not pay.

VAT return and payment dates are as for the standard scheme, unless the business is also in the annual accounting scheme.

The limits for joining and leaving this scheme are:

	VAT exclusive taxable turnover £
Join the scheme if turnover in the next 12 months is expected to be below (exclude capital supplies)	1,350,000
Leave the scheme if turnover in the previous 12 months exceeds	1,600,000

Full details of this scheme are set out in Notice 731 (July 2008) VAT: Cash Accounting.

Flat rate scheme

The scheme allows such businesses to account for VAT by applying a flat rate percentage to the business's total business supplies for a period, the result being the VAT owed to HMRC.

The main advantages of this scheme are:

- It simplifies the administration considerably, as VAT does not have to be accounted for on each individual sales and purchase invoice

- There is frequently less VAT payable to HMRC than under the normal rules

There are different flat rates set by HMRC for different trade sectors ranging from 2% to 11.5%. This percentage is applied to the **VAT inclusive** turnover of the business.

However note that there is no deduction for input VAT.

The limits for joining and leaving this scheme are:

	Turnover £
Join the scheme if TAXABLE turnover (excluding VAT) does not exceed	150,000
Leave the scheme if TOTAL turnover (including VAT) exceeds	225,000

VAT returns and payments are made as for the standard scheme.

Task 2

A trader, making standard-rated (17.5%) supplies, has joined the flat rate scheme.

The flat rate percentage applying to his business sector is 8.5%.

His VAT exclusive turnover for the quarter is £30,000.

What is the VAT due to HMRC for the quarter?

	✓
£2,550	
£2,996	

THE VAT RETURN – FLAT RATE SCHEME

Where a business accounts for VAT using the flat rate scheme there are some differences in completing the VAT return.

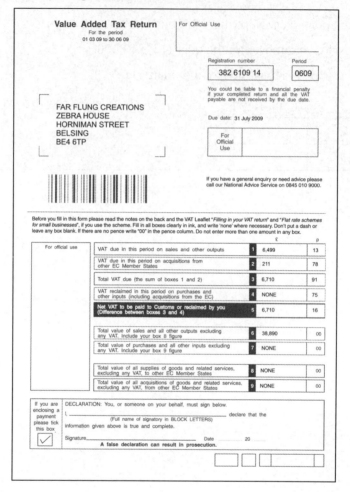

Input tax

As there is no deduction for input tax under the flat rate scheme, no figures are put into boxes 4, 7 and 9 on the return. Instead 'NONE' is entered into those boxes.

Value of sales

Boxes 6 and 8 usually contain the VAT exclusive value of sales and other outputs of the business for the period. However under the flat rate scheme the VAT INCLUSIVE figures are to be included (ie ignore the text shown at the sides of boxes 6 and 8 which ask for the VAT exclusive figures!)

CHAPTER OVERVIEW

- If a VAT-registered trader has a turnover of less than £1,350,000 excluding VAT, then he may be eligible for the annual accounting scheme – under which nine monthly direct debit payments are made based upon an estimate of the VAT liability for the year. The tenth and balancing payment is made when the VAT return for the year is submitted within two months of the year end

- If a business has an annual turnover of less than £1,350,000, excluding VAT, it may be eligible for the cash accounting scheme whereby VAT has to be accounted for to HMRC on the basis of cash payments received and made rather than on the basis of the tax point on the invoice

- If a business has an annual turnover of less than £150,000 it can simplify its VAT records by calculating its VAT payment as a percentage of total turnover instead of accounting for input and output tax on each individual purchase and sales invoice

Keywords

Annual accounting scheme – a method of accounting for VAT which does not require quarterly returns and payments – instead nine monthly direct debit payments and an annual return accompanied by the final payment

Cash accounting scheme – a method of accounting for VAT which allows VAT to be dealt with according to the date of payment or receipt of cash rather than the tax point on the invoice

Flat rate scheme – enables businesses to calculate their VAT payment as a percentage of total turnover

TEST YOUR LEARNING

Test 1

Complete the following letter to Jacob Lymstock, a client of yours who has a small business.

AN accountant
Number Street
London
SW11 8AB

Mr Lymstock
Alphabet Street
London
W12 6WM

Dear Mr Lymstock
ANNUAL ACCOUNTING SCHEME

I have recently been reviewing your files. I would like to make you aware of a scheme that you could use for VAT.

As the annual value of your taxable supplies, **(including/ excluding)** VAT and supplies of capital items, in the following 12 months is expected to be **(above/ below) £(1,350,000/1,600,000)** you can join the annual accounting scheme.

Under this scheme you make ⬚ **(insert number)** monthly direct debit payments based upon an estimate of the amount of VAT due. The first of these payments is due at the end of the ⬚ month of the accounting period. You must then prepare a VAT return for the year and send it in with the balancing payment, by **(30 days/ one month/ two months)** after the year end.

Use of this annual accounting scheme is a great help as it means that you only have to prepare ⬚ **(insert number)** VAT return(s) each year.

If you wish to discuss this with me in more detail please do not hesitate to contact me.

Your sincerely

AN Accountant

Test 2

Complete the following statement.

If the annual value of taxable supplies, **(including/ excluding)** VAT, is **(more/ less)** than £**(1,350,000/ 1,600,000)** and provided that a trader has a clean record with HMRC, he may be able to apply to use the cash accounting scheme.

The scheme allows the accounting for VAT to be based upon the date of **(receipt and payment of money/ invoice)**. This is particularly useful for a business which gives its customers a **(short/ long)** period of credit whilst paying its suppliers promptly.

The scheme also gives automatic relief from [   ] so if the customer does not pay the amount due then the VAT need not be accounted for to HMRC.

chapter 8:
ERRORS, INTEREST AND PENALTIES

chapter coverage 📖

The penalties and interest applying when VAT goes wrong have been stringently applied over many years. It is one of the reasons that many businesses who do not have to VAT register choose not to do so. The topics covered are:

- ✎ Dealing with larger errors
- ✎ Dealing with other errors
- ✎ Interest on unpaid VAT
- ✎ The effect of not sending the VAT return in on time
- ✎ Other penalties

LARGE ERRORS

If a net error of more than the greater of £10,000 and 1% of turnover, as per box 6 of the relevant return (subject to an overall £50,000 limit) is discovered it cannot be adjusted for on the VAT return.

Instead the relevant HMRC VAT Error Correction Team must be informed, in writing and preferably using Form VAT 652.

Where errors are made in VAT returns resulting in

- An understatement of the VAT liability, or
- A false or increased repayment of VAT

the penalty applied is likely to be the civil penalty of 'penalty for errors'

This penalty also applies where HMRC make an underestimated assessment of VAT due and the trader fails to notify HMRC of the error within 30 days.

The penalty is calculated as a percentage of the 'potential lost revenue'(PLR) ie the amount of the understatement or the amount of the additional reclaim. The percentage also depends on the type of error made.

A disclosure of the error will mitigate the level of any penalty.

Reason for penalty	Maximum penalty	Minimum penalty with unprompted disclosure	Minimum penalty with prompted disclosure
Deliberate and concealed action	100%	30%	50%
Deliberate but not concealed action	70%	20%	35%
Careless action	30%	Nil	15%

Examples of the types of actions are

- Deliberate and concealed

  - Creating false invoices
  - Altering invoices or other documents
  - Backdating or post-dating documents
  - Destroying books and records

- Deliberate but not concealed

  - Not keeping books and records
  - Omitting significant amounts from a return
  - Including personal expenditure in the business expenditure

- Careless
    - Keeping inaccurate or incomplete records
    - Omitting occasional items
    - Failing to check the return to the underlying records
    - Making arithmetical errors

Where an error occurs but the trader took reasonable care to get the VAT correct no penalty will apply.

OTHER ERRORS

Where errors are not deemed to be large, adjustment for them can be made on the next VAT account/ return. For example a 'small' understatement of output VAT on a previous return can be shown as an increase in the output tax on box 1 of the current return, and similarly a 'small' overstatement of input VAT on a previous return can be shown as a decrease in the input tax on box 4 of the return.

In addition the relevant HMRC VAT Error Correction Team may be informed, in writing and preferably using Form VAT 652. The box on the form should be ticked to show that the error has been adjusted for on the return.

Task 1

A business made a 'small' overstatement of input tax on a previous return. What effect will this have on the current VAT payable to HMRC?

	✓
An increase in the VAT payable via the current return	
A decrease in the VAT payable via the current return	
No impact on the current return. It must just be separately declared	

The time limit for adjusting returns and correcting errors made in previous returns, including making claims, was increased with effect from 1 April 2009 from three years to four. However, this is subject to some transitional rules, so the first time that the new four year limit will take full effect is 1 April 2010. This means that you will only need to use the old three year limit for your studies.

HOW IT WORKS

The VAT account from the earlier chapter is shown again below. Some additional items shown in italics are explained below.

VAT ACCOUNT

VAT deductible – input tax	£	VAT payable – output tax	£
VAT on purchases – from the purchases day book	3,578.90	VAT on sales – from the sales day book	5,368.70
VAT on purchases – from the cash payments book	586.73	VAT on sales – from the cash receipts book	884.56
	4,165.63		6,253.26
VAT allowable on EU acquisitions	211.78	VAT due on EU acquisitions	211.78
Net overclaim of input tax from previous returns	*–104.56*	*Net understatement of output tax on previous returns*	*287.52*
Bad debt relief	33.60	Fuel scale charge	28.15
Sub-total	4,306.45	**Sub-total**	6,780.71
Less:		Less:	
VAT on credit notes from suppliers – purchases returns day book	–49.70	VAT on credit notes to customers – sales returns day book	–69.80
Total tax deductible	4,256.75	**Total tax payable**	6,710.91
		Less: total tax deductible	–4,256.75
		Payable to HMRC	2,454.16

These entries will now be explained:

VAT deductible

- Any errors from previous VAT returns (provided that they are from accounting periods ending in the previous three years) can be adjusted for in the VAT account provided that the net value of the error does not exceed the greater of £10,000 or 1% of turnover (subject to an overall upper limit of £50,000)

- In box 4 of the VAT return, with the total of the VAT on purchases and expenses being reclaimed less the VAT on any credit notes received, any adjustments for errors relating to input VAT on previous VAT returns as mentioned above may be made

VAT payable

- The net understatement of output tax from previous periods is an error in a previous period which can be adjusted for in the VAT account provided that it is from within the last three years and it does not exceed the greater of £10,000 or 1% of turnover (subject to an overall limit of £50,000)

- In box 1 of the VAT return, with the details of the VAT on sales, less the VAT on any credit notes issued, make any adjustments for earlier period output VAT errors as mentioned above

Task 2

A business has made a small understatement of output tax in a previous quarter. Should this adjustment be shown on the latest VAT return, and if so where on the return?

	✓
No – not shown on the return	
Yes – shown in box 1	
Yes – shown in box 4	

INTEREST ON UNPAID VAT

A taxable person may be charged interest where:

- HMRC raises an assessment for under declared output tax or over claimed input tax; or
- The taxpayer voluntarily discloses a 'large' error.

Interest runs from the date the VAT should have been paid until the date that it is paid.

LATE VAT RETURN

If a business does not submit a VAT return and pay over any VAT due on the return within the stated period, (usually) one month after the end of the tax period, then that trader is in default and a SURCHARGE LIABILITY NOTICE will be sent. This warns the business that if the business defaults in respect of an accounting period within the next 12 months then a default surcharge will be issued. The surcharge is based on a percentage of the VAT that is unpaid ranging between 2% and 15%. If the business does not send in a VAT return then the amount of VAT owed will be assessed and the surcharge will be based upon this assessment.

OTHER PENALTIES

Failure to VAT register

The penalty for failing to register for VAT is worked out as a percentage of the VAT due (output tax less input tax), from the date when you should have registered to the date you inform HMRC. The percentage depends on how late you were in telling HMRC as follows:

- 5% if less than 9 months late
- 10% if 9 – 18 months late
- 15% if more than 18 months late.

This is subject to a minimum penalty of £50.

Failure to keep and retain records

As mentioned in an earlier chapter, records should be retained for six years for VAT purposes. Where records have not been retained for this period there is a maximum penalty of £3,000 per accounting period.

Fraudulent evasion of VAT

In extreme circumstances a criminal penalty may be sought when VAT evasion takes place.

Evasion of VAT includes falsely,

- Reclaiming input tax/ understating output tax
- Obtaining bad debt relief
- Obtaining a repayment

Any person who is involved in the fraudulent evasion of VAT, for himself or another person is liable

- On summary conviction, to a penalty of £5,000 or three times the amount evaded, whichever is the greater, and/ or up to six months imprisonment, or
- On conviction on indictment, to a penalty of any amount and/ or up to seven years imprisonment.

HM Revenue and Customs must prove fraud to criminal standards proof ie beyond reasonable doubt.

CHAPTER OVERVIEW

- If a net error exceeding the greater of £10,000 and 1% of turnover (subject to an overall limit of £50,000) is discovered from a previous tax period this should not be adjusted in the VAT control account – instead voluntary disclosure should be made and the VAT Business Advice Centre informed, otherwise the business might have to pay a penalty

- Interest may be payable where a large error is disclosed

- If a VAT return is late the taxpayer is served with a surcharge liability notice and may have a surcharge to pay if further late returns occur

- A number of other penalties apply for VAT purposes

Keywords

Surcharge liability notice – this warns a business that has not returned its VAT return in time that if the business defaults within the next twelve months a default surcharge will be issued

Voluntary disclosure – the method of notifying HMRC of any error found from previous returns where the error does not exceed certain limits

Evasion of VAT – falsely reclaiming input VAT/ understating output tax, obtaining bad debt relief or obtaining a repayment

TEST YOUR LEARNING

Test 1

Identify which one of the following statements is correct.

	✓
If a net error of more than the lower of £10,000 and 1% of turnover (subject to an overall £5,000 limit) is discovered it must be disclosed on Form VAT 652	
If a net error of more than the greater of £10,000 and 1% of turnover (subject to an overall £5,000 limit) is discovered it must be disclosed on Form VAT 652.	
If a net error of more than the lower of £10,000 and 1% of turnover (subject to an overall £50,000 limit) is discovered it must be disclosed on Form VAT 652.	
If a net error of more than the greater of £10,000 and 1% of turnover (subject to an overall £50,000 limit) is discovered it must be disclosed on Form VAT 652.	

Test 2

Identify whether the following statement is true or false.

If a trader fails to retain his records for at least six years the maximum penalty is £3,000 per accounting period.

True ✓	False ✓

Test 3

Given below is information about the VAT of a business taken from the books of prime entry:

From the sales day book	3,572.15
From the sales returns day book	662.70
From the purchases day book	1,825.67
From the purchases returns day book	310.56
From the cash receipts book	994.67
From the cash payments book	514.37
EU acquisitions	236.57
Bad debt relief	105.37
Output VAT underpaid in a previous period	44.79
Input VAT not reclaimed in a previous period	25.47

You are to write-up the VAT control account.

VAT ACCOUNT

VAT deductible	£	VAT payable	£
Total VAT deductible		Total VAT payable	

Picklist:

Sales day book

Sales returns day book

Purchases day book

Purchases returns day book

Cash receipts book

Cash payments book

EU acquisitions

Bad debt relief

Undercharge of output VAT

Underclaim of input VAT

Less VAT deductible

Less VAT payable

Due to HMRC

Reclaimed from HMRC

chapter 9:
CONTACT WITH CLIENTS AND HMRC

— chapter coverage 📖 —

An important part of dealing in VAT for an accountant is to be able to communicate information to both HMRC and clients, and to act professionally at all times. The topics covered are:

✎ Changes in VAT legislation and the impact on systems

✎ Seeking guidance from HMRC

CHANGES IN VAT LEGISLATION

Changes in VAT legislation are usually notified by HMRC to traders via bulletins or notices. If a change affects a certain sector of businesses then the relevant businesses will receive a paper or e-mail version of the notice.

There was a change in the standard rate of VAT from 15% to 17.5% on 1 January 2010. However, in accordance with the guidance issued by AAT, when calculating VAT you should always use a standard rate of 17.5% regardless of the date of transaction. For your assessment you simply need an awareness of how such changes can impact on businesses.

A change in the standard rate of VAT affects all VAT-registered businesses.

Impact on accounting systems

A change in the VAT rate will mean that from a certain date a different amount of VAT must be charged on certain supplies. In most situations this is fixed by the tax point. For example, when the standard rate of VAT changed from 15% to 17.5% on 1 January 2010 a standard-rated supply of £1,000 (excluding VAT) gave rise to an invoice total of £1,150 if the tax point was 31 December 2009, but £1,175 if the tax point was 1 January 2010.

The business still only receives £1,000 after paying over the output tax to HMRC.

Where a business has a computerised accounting system/tills this can give rise to problems. The systems will be set to calculate VAT at a set percentage for certain supplies. In these circumstances it is usual for the company that developed the software package to give instructions as to how the VAT rate can be changed on the system.

If a manual system is in use the trader simply needs to ensure that they are careful about applying the correct tax point for a particular supply.

Impact on customers

If customers are VAT registered then they should also be aware of changes in legislation, especially with something as significant as a change in VAT rates.

However, where customers are not VAT registered, for example in a retail business, notice should be given to customers about changes in rates. In a retail environment this would usually be via notices displayed around the store. A change in rate could impact on the charge to the customer. Using the earlier example, an item costing a customer £1,150 on 31 December 2009 would cost £1,175 on 1 January 2010 if the trader intends to have the same VAT exclusive charge. An alternative is for the trader to keep the same VAT inclusive price so that there is no impact on his customers, but this will reduce his overall turnover.

Task 1

Doug is a retailer and has been selling goods to the general public for £230 (VAT inclusive) while the VAT rate was 15%. (VAT fraction 15/115). When the VAT rate changed to 17.5% he did not want to change the cost of these goods to his customers who are not VAT registered.

Work out for Doug the VAT exclusive amount of the goods sold both before and after the change in the VAT rate.

VAT inclusive £	VAT rate	VAT exclusive £
230.00	15%	
230.00	17 ½ %	

CONTACT WITH HMRC

The main contact with HMRC for a VAT-registered person is the National Advice Service (NAS). They are able to advise registered persons on most VAT matters and they also keep stocks of VAT publications.

The telephone number of the NAS can be found on the HMRC web site.

Whenever a registered person contacts the NAS in writing or by telephone they should always quote their VAT registration number, and keep a note of the conversation and the call reference given.

In assessments, you will typically be required to seek guidance from the NAS in writing on some aspect of the organisation's affairs. The area that you have to enquire about may be very simple or it may be more complicated or obscure. If it is a simple point then the task may require a brief explanation of the point as well as seeking more detailed guidance from the NAS. If the point is more complex then you will only be required to ask for guidance in an intelligent and professional manner, not to understand the sometimes complex provisions of VAT law.

The NAS asks that anyone with a query refers to the relevant public notice first to try to answer their question. If the enquirer, having done this, is still not confident of the situation, NAS will answer a written query.

Applications for clearance

Businesses can apply for 'clearance' where there is significant uncertainty about the tax consequences of transactions affecting their business.

Normally, for VAT clearances, it is the supplier who should ask for a clearance on a liability to tax of goods or services. However, the clearance should not vary in circumstances where the same question and facts are set out by the recipient of the supply. If the enquiry relates to tax recovery, then it is the recipient of the supply who should make the clearance application.

Applications can be sent by post to the HMRC Clearances Team.

Visits from HMRC

From time to time an HMRC officer will visit a VAT registered business in order to examine the business records and accounting methods, and to determine whether the correct amount of VAT has been paid and whether returns are completed on time.

Usually there will be a set date agreed with the officer for the visit but on occasions an officer may arrive unannounced in order to see the day to day operations of the business.

If the officer believes that VAT has been underpaid, HMRC will raise an assessment requesting payment of the VAT due. If the trader disagrees with the assessment, an appeals procedure is in place to deal with the dispute.

CONTACTING HMRC AND CLIENTS

For assessment criteria 2.2 and 2.3 (Preparing and completing VAT returns), candidates are required to communicate effectively with clients or HMRC. Whenever contact is made with the NAS or with HMRC officers this must always be done in a polite and professional manner. Similarly, a professional approach should also be adopted with clients and other colleagues.

CHAPTER OVERVIEW

- Changes in VAT legislation can have significant impact on accounting systems

- The main contact for advice and help for any VAT-registered business is the local National Advice Service

Keywords

National Advice Service – the VAT helpline able to deal with general enquiries and to give advice

Clearance – a system for business to ask how tax law will apply to a specific transaction/series of transactions

TEST YOUR LEARNING

Test 1

You are a trainee accounting technician working for a sole trader, Mr Smith. Mr Smith has just received a letter from a client, Michael James, who is a trader making only standard-rated supplies to non-registered clients, asking about the impact of the recent change in the standard rate of VAT on his clients. He is undecided about whether to change his prices.

You are required to draft a letter to Michael James discussing the options open to him.

CHAPTER 1   The VAT system

Task 1

	Input tax ✓	Output tax ✓
Business A		✓
Business B	✓	

Task 2

	✓
Telephone calls from home phone of £28 (including VAT)	
Purchases of snacks costing £10 (including VAT) from a shop for a business meeting	
Multi storey car parking charges of £21 (including VAT)	✓
Purchases of pens and pencils using petty cash of £18 (including VAT)	

No VAT invoice required for expenditure on:

- Telephone calls from public or private telephones
- Purchases through coin operated machines
- Car park charges

provided that they are for £25 or less including the VAT.

CHAPTER 2   Accounting for VAT

Task 1

The correct three items that must be included on a valid VAT invoice are:

- Supplier VAT registration number
- Total VAT exclusive amount
- Total VAT amount

Task 2

	✓
Input tax will increase	✓
Input tax will decrease	
Output tax will increase	
Output tax will decrease	

CHAPTER 3   Types of supply

Task 1

The correct answers are:

Business type	Type of supply made	Net cost £
Insurance company	Only exempt supplies	1,175
Accountancy firm	Only standard rated supplies	1,000
Bus company	Only zero rated supplies	1,000

Although the accountancy firm and bus company pay £1,175 for their telephone bills, they are able to reclaim the input VAT of £175, so the net cost is £1,000. The insurance company making exempt supplies is not able to reclaim input tax and so the net cost is £1,175.

Task 2

To registered traders	To non-registered traders	✓
Zero-rated	Zero-rated	
Standard-rated	Zero-rated	
Zero-rated	Standard-rated	✓
Standard-rated	Standard-rated	

CHAPTER 4   VAT registration and deregistration

Task 1

VAT registration is required when TAXABLE supplies (standard plus zero-rated supplies) exceed £68,000. Taxable supplies are £7,920 (£6,850 +£1,070) per month.

After nine months, ie by 30 April 2009, taxable supplies are £71,280 (9 × £7,920) therefore Amy must apply to HMRC by 30 days after this, ie by 30 May 2009.

The correct answer is 30 May 2009.

CHAPTER 5   Output tax and input tax

Task 1

VAT exclusive	VAT rate	VAT	VAT inclusive
£	%	£	£
43.50	17.5	7.61	51.11
18.00	5	0.90	18.90

VAT = £51.11 × 7/47   VAT = £18.90 ×1/21

    = £7.61   = £0.90

Task 2

	✓
15 May 2009	
20 May 2009	✓
20 June 2009	

Basic tax point	15 May 2009
Invoice date	20 May 2009
Payment date	20 June 2009
Is payment or invoice earlier than basic tax point?	No – so this does not create an actual tax point
Is invoice within 14 days of basic tax point?	Yes – so invoice date overrides basic tax point
TAX POINT	**20 May – actual**

Task 3

	✓
2 June 2009	✓
11 June 2009	✓
29 June 2009	
31 July 2009	

Tax point

	10% deposit	*Balancing payment*
Basic tax point	11 June 2009	11 June 2009
Invoice date	29 June 2009	29 June 2009
Payment date	2 June 2009	31 July 2009
Is payment or invoice earlier than basic tax point?	Yes – payment 2 June 2009	No – both later
Is invoice within 14 days of basic tax point?	No	No
TAX POINT	**2 June 2009 – actual**	**11 June 2009 – basic**

Task 4

	✓
£175.00	
£171.50	
£140.00	
£137.20	✓

	£
Goods total	1,000
Less: trade discount	200
	800
Less: settlement discount	16
VAT £784.00 × 17.5% = £137.20	784

Task 5

	✓
The amount payable will increase	
The amount payable will decrease	✓

CHAPTER 6   VAT return

Task 1

	✓
Input tax paid at the ports is reclaimed as input tax on the VAT return	
They are shown as both input tax and output tax on the VAT return	✓
They are zero rated and so do not feature on the VAT return	
They are exempt and so do not feature on the VAT return	

Task 2

To: Finance Director
From: Accounting Technician
Date: 25 April 20XX
Subject: VAT return to 31 March 20XX

Please be advised that I have now completed the VAT return for the quarter
to 31 March 20XX. If you are in agreement with the figures shown in the
return please could you arrange an electronic payment of **£2,062.08**
to be made by **7 May 20XX**.

If you wish to discuss this further please feel free to call me.

Kind regards

CHAPTER 7   Schemes for small businesses

Task 1

	True	False
The first payment due to HMRC is by 1 April 2010.		✓

The first payment due to HMRC is by 30 April 2010 (ie the END of month 4).

Task 2

	✓
£2,550	
£2,996	✓

The VAT due to HMRC is 8.5% of the VAT inclusive figure.

$(£30,000 \times 117.5\%) \times 8.5\% = £2,996$

CHAPTER 8   Errors, interest and penalties

Task 1

	✓
An increase in the VAT payable via the current return	✓
A decrease in the VAT payable via the current return	
No impact on the current return. It must just be separately declared	

Task 2

	✓
No – not shown on the return	
Yes – shown in box 1	✓
Yes – shown in box 4	

It is shown as an increase in the output tax at box 1 on the VAT return.

CHAPTER 9   Contact with clients and HMRC

Task 1

VAT inclusive £	VAT rate	VAT exclusive £
230.00	15%	200.00
230.00	17 ½ %	195.74

- VAT rate of 15% (VAT fraction 15/115)

  VAT exclusive value £200 (100/115 × £230)
- VAT rate of 17.5% (VAT fraction 17.5/117.5)

  VAT exclusive value £195.74 (100/117.5 × £230)

TEST YOUR LEARNING – ANSWERS

CHAPTER 1   The VAT system

Test 1

	✓
HM Customs and Excise	
Inland Revenue	
HM Revenue and Customs	✓
HM Treasury	

Test 2

	✓
Output VAT is the VAT charged by a supplier on the sales that are made by his business. Output VAT is collected by the supplier and paid over to HMRC.	✓
Output VAT is the VAT suffered by the purchaser of the goods which will be reclaimed from HMRC if the purchaser is VAT registered and a valid VAT invoice is held.	

The other statement describes input VAT.

Test 3

VAT is collected by HMRC throughout the manufacturing chain for goods. Each business that buys, processes and then sells the goods pays the difference between the VAT on their sale and the VAT on their purchase over to HMRC.

Test 4

	✓
1 year	
2 years	
6 years	✓
20 years	

Test 5

	True ✓	False ✓
Copies of sales invoices do not need to be kept		✓
Supplier invoices must be kept as evidence of input VAT incurred	✓	

Copies of sales invoices must be kept as evidence of output tax charged.

Supplier invoices must be kept in order to reclaim input VAT.

CHAPTER 2   Accounting for VAT

Test 1

	✓
A pro forma invoice is always sent out when goods are sent to customers, before issuing the proper invoice	
A pro forma invoice always includes the words 'This is not a VAT invoice'	✓
A customer can reclaim VAT stated on a pro forma invoice	
A pro forma invoice is sent out to offer a customer the chance to purchase the goods detailed	✓

Test 2

VAT CONTROL ACCOUNT

VAT deductible	£	VAT payable	£
Purchases day book	6,344.03	Sales day book	9,147.96
Cash payments book	936.58	Cash receipts book	1,662.78
	7,280.61		10,810.74
Purchases returns day book	663.57	Sales returns day book	994.67
Total VAT deductible	6,617.04	Total VAT payable	9,816.07
		Less: VAT deductible	6,617.04
		Due to HMRC	3,199.03

CHAPTER 3   Types of supply

Test 1

17.5	%
5	%
0	%

Standard rate, reduced rate and zero rate.

Test 2

	True ✓	False ✓
If a business supplies zero rated services then the business is not able to reclaim the VAT on its purchases and expenses from HMRC.		✓
A business makes zero rated supplies. The cost to the business of its purchases and expenses is the VAT exclusive amount.	✓	

Test 3

	✓
The goods will be treated as standard rated in the UK if the American business is VAT registered	
The goods will be treated as standard rated in the UK provided documentary evidence of the export is obtained within 3 months	
The goods will be treated as zero rated in the UK if the American business is VAT registered	
The goods will be treated as zero rated in the UK provided documentary evidence of the export is obtained within 3 months	✓

CHAPTER 4   VAT registration and deregistration

Test 1

AN Accountant
Number Street
London
SW11 8AB

Mrs Quirke
Alphabet Street
London
W12 6WM

Dear Mrs Quirke
VAT REGISTRATION

Further to our recent telephone conversation, set out below are the circumstances when you must register your business for VAT.

If the taxable turnover of your business for the prior period, but not looking back more than **twelve** months, has exceeded the registration limit of **£68,000**, then the business must apply to register within **30 days** of the end of that period. It will be registered from **one month and one day** after the end of the relevant month.

Alternatively, if at any time, the taxable turnover (before any VAT is added) is expected to exceed the annual registration limit within the next **30 days** , then the business must apply within **30 days** to be registered for VAT, but is registered from **the beginning of the 30-day period**. This would be the situation if, for example, you obtained a large one-off contract for, say, £70,000.

If you wish to discuss this in any more detail please do not hesitate to contact me.

Yours sincerely

AN Accountant

CHAPTER 5   Output tax and input tax

Test 1

(a)

The VAT is £	67.20

VAT =   £384.00 × 17.5%

=   £67.20

(b)   Which business will treat it as output tax and which will treat it as input tax?

	Output tax ✓	Input tax ✓
Business C	✓	
Business D		✓

Test 2

	✓
Diaries for staff	
Car for sales manager	✓
Photocopier	
Entertaining clients	✓

Test 3

	Date	Basic/ Actual
An invoice is sent out to a customer for goods on 22 June 2009 and the goods are dispatched on 29 June 2009	22 June	A
Goods are sent out to a customer on 18 June 2009 and this is followed by an invoice on 23 June 2009	23 June	A
A customer pays in full for goods on 27 June 2009 and they are then delivered to the customer on 2 July 2009.	27 June	A

Test 4

	£
A VAT exclusive list price of £356.79 will have VAT of	62.43
A VAT exclusive list price of £269.00 where a trade discount of 15 % is given will have VAT of	40.01
A VAT exclusive list price of £250.00 where a 2.5% settlement discount is offered will have VAT of	42.65
A VAT exclusive list price of £300.00 where a trade discount of 10% is given and a 3% settlement discount is offered will have VAT of	45.83

(i)   £356.79 × 17.5%   =   £62.43

(ii)   (£269.00 – £40.35) × 17.5%   =   £40.01

(iii)   (£250.00 – £6.25) × 17.5%   =   £42.65

(iv)   (£300.00 – £30.00 – £8.10) × 17.5%   =   £45.83

Test 5

VAT inclusive £	VAT at 17 ½ % £
42.88	6.38
96.35	14.35
28.20	4.20
81.07	12.07

(i)   £42.88 × 7/47   =   £6.38

(ii)   £96.35 × 7/47   =   £14.35

(iii)   £28.20 × 7/47   =   £4.20

(iv)   £81.07 × 7/47   =   £12.07

Test 6

The VAT on a bad debt can be reclaimed from HMRC when the following three conditions are met:

- The debt is more than six months overdue
- The original VAT on the invoice has been paid to HMRC
- The debt is written-off in the accounts of the business

CHAPTER 6   VAT return

Test 1

WORKINGS	£
Box 1	
VAT on sales from the sales day book	7,921.80
VAT on sales from the cash receipts book	884.56
Less: VAT on credit notes issued	(135.37)
	8,670.99
Box 2	
VAT on EU acquisitions	394.81
Box 4	
VAT on purchases from purchases day book	5,359.82
VAT on purchases from cash payments book	586.73
VAT on EU acquisitions	394.81
Less: VAT on credit notes received	(124.98)
	6,216.38
Box 6	
Zero-rated credit sales	13,447
Standard-rated credit sales	45,267
Cash sales	5,054
Less: zero-rated credit notes	(225)
standard-rated credit notes	(773)
	62,770
Box 7	
Zero-rated credit purchases	7,447
Standard-rated credit purchases	30,627
Cash purchases	3,352
EU acquisitions	2,256
Less: zero rated credit notes	(215)
standard-rated credit notes	(714)
	42,753
Box 9	
Purchases from EU countries	2,256

VAT due in this period on **sales** and other outputs (Box 1) | 8,670.99

VAT due in this period on **acquisitions** from other **EC Member States** (Box 2) | 394.81

Total VAT due (**the sum of boxes 1 and 2**) (Box 3) | 9,065.80

VAT reclaimed in the period on **purchases** and other inputs, including acquisitions from the EC (Box 4) | 6,216.38

Net VAT to be paid to HM Revenue & Customs or reclaimed by you (**Difference between boxes 3 and 4**) (Box 5) | 2,849.42

Total value of **sales** and all other outputs excluding any VAT. **Include your box 8 figure** (Box 6) | 62,770
Whole pounds only

Total value of purchases and all other inputs excluding any VAT. **Include your box 9 figure** (Box 7) | 42,754
Whole pounds only

Total value of all **supplies** of goods and related costs, excluding any VAT, to other **EC Member States** (Box 8) | None
Whole pounds only

Total value of all **acquisitions** of goods and related costs, excluding any VAT, from other **EC Member States** (Box 9) | 2,256
Whole pounds only

CHAPTER 7   Schemes for small businesses

Test 1

AN accountant
Number Street
London
SW11 8AB

Mr Lymstock
Alphabet Street
London
W12 6WM

Dear Mr Lymstock
ANNUAL ACCOUNTING SCHEME

I have recently been reviewing your files. I would like to make you aware of a scheme that you could use for VAT.

As the annual value of your taxable supplies, **excluding** VAT and supplies of capital items, in the following 12 months is expected to be **below £1,350,000** you can join the annual accounting scheme.

Under this scheme you make **9** monthly direct debit payments based upon an estimate of the amount of VAT due. The first of these payments is due at the end of the **fourth** month of the accounting period. You must then prepare a VAT return for the year and send it in with the balancing payment, by **two months** after the year end.

Use of this annual accounting scheme is a great help as it means that you only have to prepare **one** VAT return(s) each year.

If you wish to discuss this with me in more detail please do not hesitate to contact me.

Your sincerely

AN Accountant

Test 2

If the annual value of taxable supplies, **excluding** VAT, is **less** than **£1,350,000** and provided that a trader has a clean record with HMRC, he may be able to apply to use the cash accounting scheme.

The scheme allows the accounting for VAT to be based upon the date of **receipt and payment of money**. This is particularly useful for a business which gives its customers a **long** period of credit whilst paying its suppliers promptly.

The scheme also gives automatic relief from **bad debts** so if the customer does not pay the amount due then the VAT need not be accounted for to HMRC.

CHAPTER 8   Errors, interest and penalties

Test 1

The correct statement is:

	✓
If a net error of more than the lower of £10,000 and 1% of turnover (subject to an overall £5,000 limit) is discovered it must be disclosed on Form VAT 652	
If a net error of more than the greater of £10,000 and 1% of turnover (subject to an overall £5,000 limit) is discovered it must be disclosed on Form VAT 652.	
If a net error of more than the lower of £10,000 and 1% of turnover (subject to an overall £50,000 limit) is discovered it must be disclosed on Form VAT 652.	
If a net error of more than the greater of £10,000 and 1% of turnover (subject to an overall £50,000 limit) is discovered it must be disclosed on Form VAT 652.	✓

Test 2

True	False
✓	✓
✓	

Test 3

VAT CONTROL ACCOUNT

VAT deductible	£	VAT payable	£
Purchases day book	1,825.67	Sales day book	3,572.15
Cash payments book	514.37	Cash receipts book	994.67
EU acquisitions	236.57	EU acquisitions	236.57
Bad debt relief	105.37	Undercharge of output VAT	44.79
Underclaim of input VAT	25.47		
	2,707.45		4,848.18
Purchases returns day book	310.56	Sales returns day book	662.70
Total VAT deductible	2,396.89	Total VAT payable	4,185.48
		Less: VAT deductible	−2,396.89
		Due to HMRC	1,788.59

CHAPTER 9   Contact with clients and HMRC

Test 1

Mr Smith
Number Street
London
SW11 8AB

Mr James
Alphabet Street
London
W12 6WM

Dear Mr James
CHANGE IN THE STANDARD RATE OF VAT

Further to your recent letter, I have set out below the options open to you in relation to the recent change in the standard rate of VAT.

Until recently you have been charging VAT at a rate of 15%. Therefore a VAT exclusive sale with a value of £1,000 has cost your non-registered clients £1,150 (£1,000 plus VAT of £150).

The two options open to you are as follows:

- Keep the same VAT exclusive value of £1,000

  The benefit of this option is that you have the same amount of VAT exclusive sales value per item sold. However, this will now make the VAT inclusive cost to your customers higher at £1,175 (£1,000 plus VAT at 17.5%). This makes your prices less competitive and may result in a loss of some customers.

- Keep the same VAT inclusive value of £1,150

  Under this alternative option you will remain competitive to your customers. However, your VAT exclusive sales value per item sold will be reduced to £978.72 (£1,150 × 100/117.5).

There is no obvious correct option to choose, it will depend primarily on the strength of your competitors.

If you wish to discuss this with me in more detail please do not hesitate to contact me.

Your sincerely

Mr Smith

INDEX

Notes

Notes

REVIEW FORM

How have you used this Text?
(Tick one box only)

☐ Home study

☐ On a course_____

☐ Other _____

Why did you decide to purchase this Text?
(Tick one box only)

☐ Have used BPP Texts in the past

☐ Recommendation by friend/colleague

☐ Recommendation by a college lecturer

☐ Saw advertising

☐ Other _____

During the past six months do you recall seeing/receiving either of the following?
(Tick as many boxes as are relevant)

☐ Our advertisement in Accounting Technician

☐ Our Publishing Catalogue

Which (if any) aspects of our advertising do you think are useful?
(Tick as many boxes as are relevant)

☐ Prices and publication dates of new editions

☐ Information on Text content

☐ Details of our free online offering

☐ None of the above

Your ratings, comments and suggestions would be appreciated on the following areas of this Text.

	Very useful	Useful	Not useful
Introductory section	☐	☐	☐
Quality of explanations	☐	☐	☐
How it works	☐	☐	☐
Chapter tasks	☐	☐	☐
Chapter Overviews	☐	☐	☐
Test your learning	☐	☐	☐
Index	☐	☐	☐

	Excellent	Good	Adequate	Poor
Overall opinion of this Text	☐	☐	☐	☐

Do you intend to continue using BPP Products?   ☐ Yes   ☐ No

Please note any further comments and suggestions/errors on the reverse of this page. The author of this edition can be e-mailed at: suedexter@bpp.com

Please return to: Sue Dexter, Publishing Director, BPP Learning Media Ltd, FREEPOST, London, W12 8BR.

REVIEW FORM (continued)

TELL US WHAT YOU THINK

Please note any further comments and suggestions/errors below.